Westercon 70 Program Guide

ISBN-10: 0-9894613-5-1

ISBN-13: 978-0-9894613-5-1

Cover art is *Skyward Bound* by Artist GoH Julie Dillon
http://www.juliedillonart.com/

'Westercon' is a registered service mark of the
Los Angeles Science Fantasy Society, Inc.

Westercon 70

Saturday July 1 to Tuesday July 4, 2017, plus pre- and post-con events
Tempe Mission Palms, 60 E 5th St, Tempe, AZ 85281

Chair: Dee Astell

Treasurer: Kevin McAlonan

Leprecon, Inc.

Our sponsoring body, Leprecon, Inc., is a 501(c)(3) non-profit.
PO Box 26665, Tempe, AZ 85285-6665 | leprecon.org/corp

Chairman: Paul Tanton

Secretary: Kevin McAlonan

Treasurer: Bruce Farr

Program Guide Editor: Hal C. F. Astell

Typeset in Gentium Plus
http://software.sil.org/gentium/

Published through CreateSpace
https://www.createspace.com/

ISBN donated by Apocalypse Later Press
https://www.apocalypselaterempire.com/al/alp/

Any ongoing proceeds from the sale of this Program Guide
on Amazon will go in entirety to Leprecon, Inc.

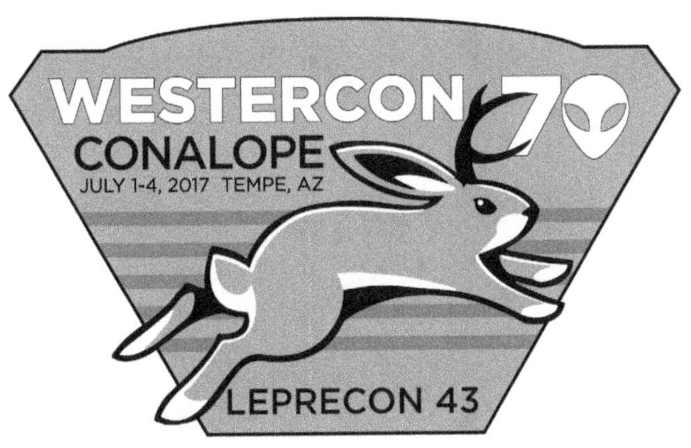

Westercon 70 Program Guide

Please welcome our Guests of Honor:

Julie Dillon, Tom Deadstuff
Connie Willis, Gini Koch
Val & Ron Ontell, Tim Griffin, Henry Vanderbilt
Larry Elmore, Bjo & John Trimble
Weston Ochse

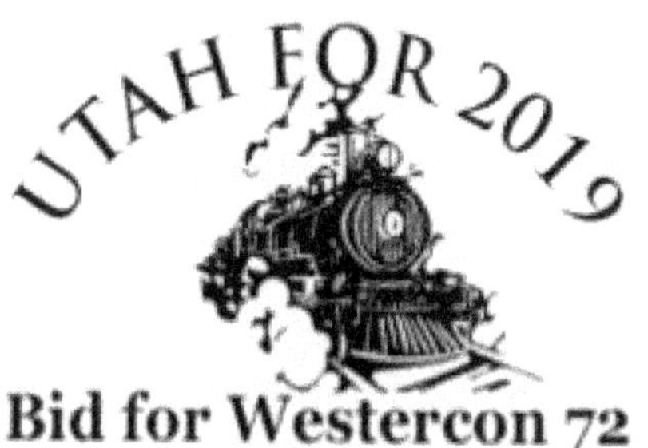

Bid for Westercon 72

Layton City, Utah
Davis Conference Center & Hilton Garden Inn
July 4th - 7th, 2019

SCIENCE FICTION. FANTASY. ART. STEAMPUNK.
GAMING. ANIME. COSTUMING. POETRY & MORE.

Westercon 72 Bid

NASFiC 2019 Bid

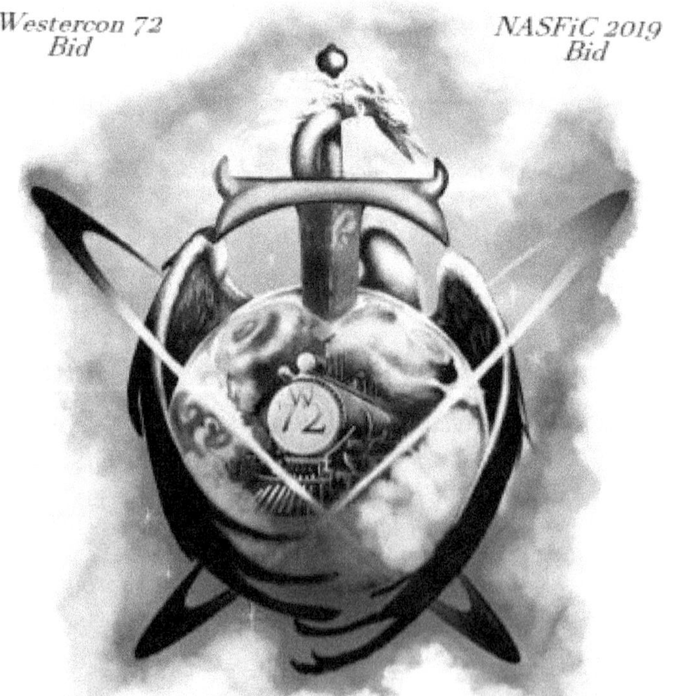

OUR GOAL NEEDS ONE MORE MAJOR INGREDIENT: YOU!

FIND & PRE-SUPPORT US ONLINE AT: UTAHFOR2019.COM · INFO@UTAHFOR2019.COM

Dedication

We dedicate this program book to all those who created, built and maintained Arizona fandom over the past half century, especially those who are no longer with us.

We walk in your footprints as best we can.

Acknowledgements

We thank our sponsoring body, Leprecon, Inc. for backing our bid and making this Westercon possible.

We thank the legions who have contributed to Westercon 70 as staff, minions, participants, volunteers, donators, sponsors and any other roles that may have briefly slipped past us.

We also thank Mike Willmoth, former Chairman of Leprecon, Inc. (and Chair of Westercon 62) for his time, energy and dedication, not to mention patience over a decade, as he moves upward and onward.

Contents

Key Locations

A map of the Tempe Mission Palms is on the back cover.

Art Show - Palm B/C
Author Readings - Boardroom
Autograph Sessions - Cloister
Blood Drive Signup - Foyer
Business Meeting - Sand Lotus
Charity Auction - Cloister
ConSuite - Suite 2038
Dealers' Room - Palm A/D
Events - mostly Palm E/F
Fannish Inquisition - Sand Lotus
Fan Tables - Foyer
Filk Room - Joshua Tree
Film Festival - Wind Flower
Gaming Hall - Abbey
Info Desk - Colonnade
Lost and Found - Colonnade
Masquerade Green Room - Dolores
Operations - Colonnade
Registration - Lobby
Site Selection - Foyer

Guests and Sponsors

Please support our Guests of Honor and our Sponsors, who made it possible for us to make this convention happen.

Guests of Honor:

Artist:	Julie Dillon	juliedillonart.com
Local Artist:	Tom Deadstuff	tomdeadstuff.com
Author:	Connie Willis	sftv.org/cw
Local Author:	Gini Koch	ginikoch.com
Fen:	Val & Ron Ontell	ontell.org
Filk:	Tim Griffin	griffined.org
Science:	Henry Vanderbilt	space-access.org
Special Artist:	Larry Elmore	larryelmore.com
Special Media:	Bjo & John Trimble	facebook.com/thetrimbles
Toastmaster:	Weston Ochse	westonochse.com

Guest of Honor Sponsors:

Larry Elmore	LepreCon 44	leprecon.org
Tim Griffin	Phoenix Filk Circle	
The Trimbles	United Federation of Phoenix	u-f-p.org
Connie Willis	WesternSFA	westernsfa.org

Other Sponsors:

Sponsoring Body	Leprecon, Inc.	leprecon.org/corp
Ice Cream Social	Baen Books	baen.com
Swag Bags/Books	DAW Books	penguin.com/publishers/daw
Books	Del Rey Books	randomhousebooks.com
Maps/Guides	Arizona Office of Tourism	tourism.az.gov
Candy Dishes, Swag for At the Movies	CASFS	casfs.org
Art/Craft Supplies	Arizona Penny Dreadfuls	azpennydreadfuls.org
Program Book ISBN	Apocalypse Later Press	apocalypselaterempire.com/al/alp

Message from the Chair

I want to thank you for joining us at this year's Westercon. We share a 70th anniversary with the arrival of *something* in Roswell, NM, hence our theme. We believe that the stranded aliens wrangled a horde of frisky jackalopes and rode northwest to Tempe. Who knows, you might spot an alien or even an elusive jackalope running around the hotel this weekend!

Our staff have worked very hard to bring you the best programming and make this event one to remember. I thank you all. I couldn't have done this without you.

As Countess Chaos, I'm especially fond of the steampunk genre and we've brought you a lot of that this weekend, but we also have a strong authors track, a focus on science and education and much more.

I would like to thank our Guests of Honor for spending their valuable time here in Arizona with us, especially given that it's July.

As we're sponsored by Leprecon, Inc., I decided to make this not just Westercon 70 but also LepreCon 43, our local sci-fi/fantasy convention that has had a special focus on art for the past three decades. We're also including CONflagration, a former standalone gaming convention that has been the gaming track for the last few LepreCons. We're keeping that alive at Westercon 70 too.

I hope you find the opportunity to check out some of the special events that we've brought to you, including some Westercon favorites but also some Arizona traditions too, like Evening Erotica with Gini Koch and Body Painting with Mark Greenawalt, like Len Berger's At the Movies and Hal's Apocalypse Later mini-film festival. Cathy Book always runs a fantastic Charity Auction and this one may be her biggest yet.

I'm particularly proud to have been able to bring so many of our Arizona fandom groups into Westercon 70 as active participants, sponsors, staff members and party hosts. This is one community and it's great to see all the groups working together.

— Dee Astell
Chair, Westercon 70

What is Westercon?

What is Westercon? Westercon is the West Coast Science Fantasy Conference, held annually since 1948 in the western half of North America (including Hawaii). It is a general interest science fiction and fantasy convention covering literature, art, science, costuming, gaming, music, television, movies and any other topic of interest to sf/f fans. Please visit westercon.org for more details.

When is Westercon held? Westercon is traditionally held over the 4th of July weekend, although this is not mandatory.

Where is Westercon held? It has been held from Hawaii to Spokane, from El Paso to Seattle. Last year, it was in Portland, OR. This year, it's in Tempe, AZ. Next year, it will be in Westminster, CO. The only bid for 2019 is for Layton, UT.

Who runs Westercon? Different non-profit groups run Westercon every year, since the event moves from city to city. In 2017, it will be run by volunteers from around Arizona and beyond, sponsored by Leprecon, Inc., a 501(c)(3) non-profit. Please visit leprecon.org/corp for more details.

Why is Westercon held? Although it was started for those fans who couldn't afford to travel to the east coast to attend the World Science Fiction Convention (Worldcon), it's become an event for fans from around North America to travel to different parts of the West, to communicate with different communities and experience the flavor of the region, not only regarding science fiction and fantasy.

How does it work? A non-profit group expresses interest in hosting a Westercon, be they in Los Angeles or Portland or wherever. They bid for the event starting about four years out, or two years prior to the vote. If they win the bid, then they have two years to organize it. They must have a site (usually a hotel) and a committee or team to run the event. They invite professionals and fans of note to speak and present and advertise to draw in the fandom community.

Fandom Cheat Sheet

As a traditional science fiction/fantasy con, Westercon 70 follows many science fiction/fantasy con traditions. If you're new to these, they may seem strange, so here's a cheat sheet to guide you through such traditions.

Bid Party - A party, usually on the 'Party Floor' held by those who have bid to host a future event (like a Westercon) and want to get the word out. If a bid party door is open, you're welcome to enter for free food, drink or company. It's courteous to ask about a bid, but you don't have to support.

ConSuite - A hotel room where attendees can visit, eat (for free), find good conversation and a place to relax. Our ConSuite is in suite 2038.

Dead Dog - At the end of a convention, when all the programming has finished, there's a final party (and maybe filk session) for those fans who know it's all over but don't want to go home yet.

Filk - Songs with a science fiction and fantasy focus that are often set to familiar tunes. Joshua Tree is our dedicated filk room at Westercon 70. Open filk sessions are when anyone can join in. Tim Griffin is our Filk GoH.

GoHs - Guests of Honor are individuals of note that the convention (or its sponsors) have chosen to honor by bringing them out to be a special focus. Please make them especially welcome.

Hall Costumes - Costumes worn while walking the halls of the con, not just at the Masquerade. Secret judges may award hall costume prizes.

Masquerade - A pageant event, somewhere in between a fashion show and a costume contest, in which contestants show off costumes that they have created themselves and perform short skits.

Meet the Guests - An opportunity to mingle and chat with our GoHs. Ours is an Ice Cream Social on Saturday afternoon in the ConSuite.

Past GoHs - People who have been honored at previous LepreCon or Westercon events. They may wear a Past GoH con ribbon on their badge.

Room Party - A party held in the evening, usually on the 'Party Floor', held for no reason other than to hold a party. If a room party door is open, you're welcome to enter for free food, drink and company.

Guest of Honor Appreciations

Please join us in welcoming our Guests of Honor to Westercon 70!

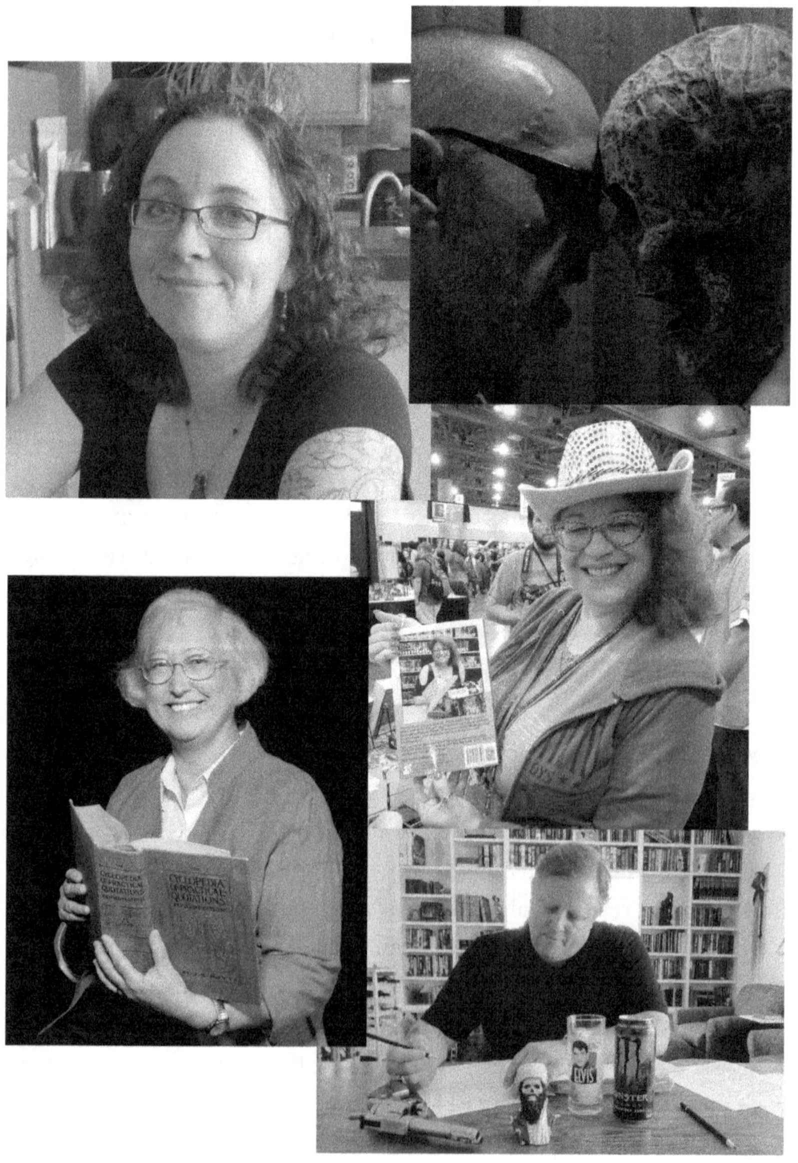

Opposite (clockwise from top left): Julie Dillon, Tom Deadstuff, Gini Koch, Weston Ochse, Connie Willis. This page (clockwise from top left): Val & Ron Ontell, Henry Vanderbilt, John & Bjo Trimble, Larry Elmore, Tim Griffin

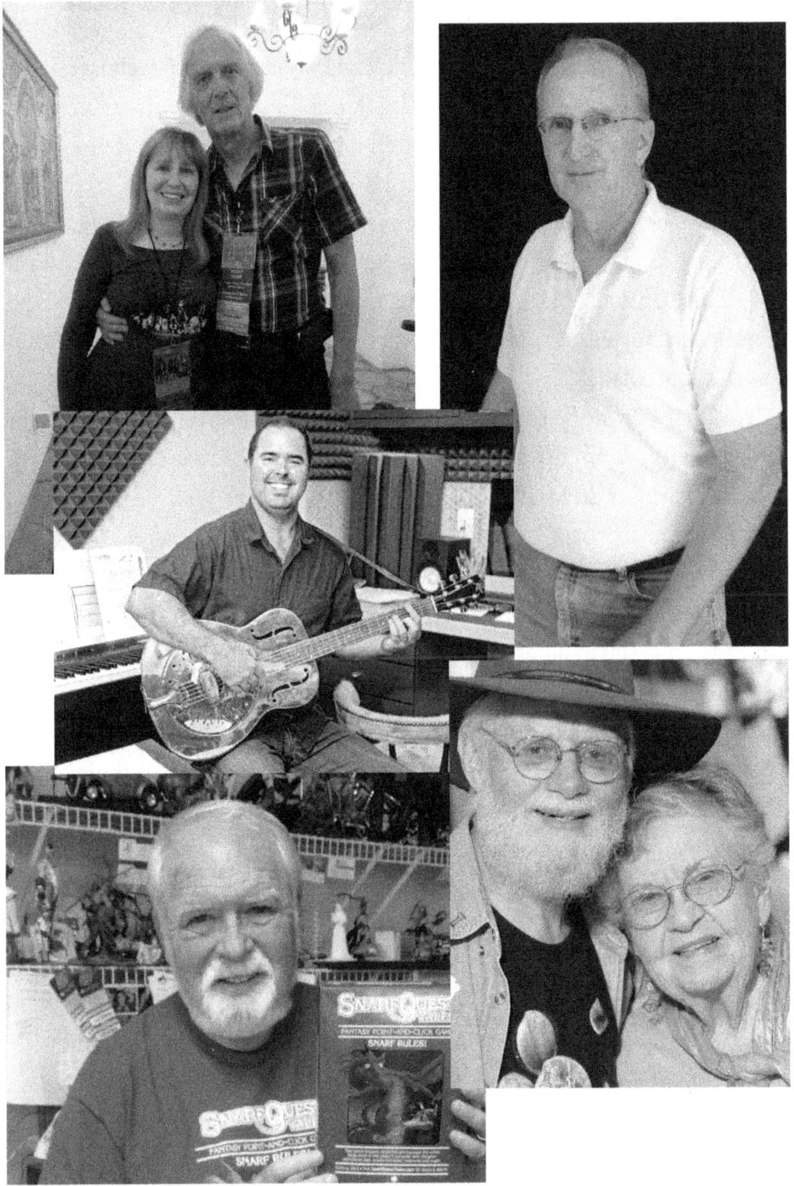

Artist GoH: Julie Dillon

When I was asked to write an introduction for Julie Dillon, I must admit, I was unfamiliar with her work. This does not reflect poorly on her, but is a rather sad commentary on my own lack of awareness in my chosen field. Julie is living the life of a successful freelance illustrator, which, combined with novel writing, is what I most often dream about for myself. Her work has been used for book and magazine covers, trading cards, and even perfume labels. Honored over a dozen times by the fantasy and sci-fi publishing industry, she was nominated Best Artist for the World Fantasy Award in 2012 and 2014, is a four-time Chesley Award winner, and won the Hugo Award for Best Professional Artist two years in a row, to name but a few of her accolades.

It was her artwork that caught my attention however, not her list of achievements. I immediately noticed the 'Art Nouveau' influences of illustrator Alphonse Mucha in the flowing, billowing lines of her figures, juxtaposed with the geometric framing of circles and graceful, organic curves. Her use of vibrant color was striking; many pieces reminded me of the lushest of Maxfield Parrish lightscapes, but with the saturated intensity of electric blues, ultra-violets, radiant reds, and the rest of the digital enhanced chromatic spectrum. Contrasting colors run blazing hot and icy cold, making the virtual canvas resonate. When she uses monochromatic palettes, her images manage to lose none of their depth and intensity. The emotional influence of color is brought out as its saturation, lightness, and temperature are explored and exploited.

But what impressed me most, more so because I have no great or small talent for it myself, was the use of surrealism and dreamlike imagery present in most of her compositions. Being a fantasy artist requires a mind not only for the unusual or unlikely, but the truly fantastic. Julie's work is nothing if not fantastic, to use the proper, more archaic definition. Worlds cluster together like islands in a celestial ocean; flat, planar clouds of mist hang in the air like sheets of stained glass; giant orreries twist and turn with polished copper brilliance; golden clockwork fish swim through an azure atmosphere; celestial figures merge with the landscape and the elements, dwarfing the tiny mortal figures below.

One of the great joys of being introduced to something marvelous and new is the way it drives one's mind in different, unplanned directions. The art of fantasy and science fiction have a way of doing this more than other genres, for by their nature, they are pushing the boundaries of our thoughts and perceptions. Julie Dillon is yet another fine artist that I have had the pleasure of being exposed to on my journey and her vision has led me to think in new directions, challenging me to break out of my bubble and explore fresh ideas. This is perhaps the highest praise I can offer to a fellow creator, and a gift that all artists hope to share with others.

— Mark Rude
author and artist

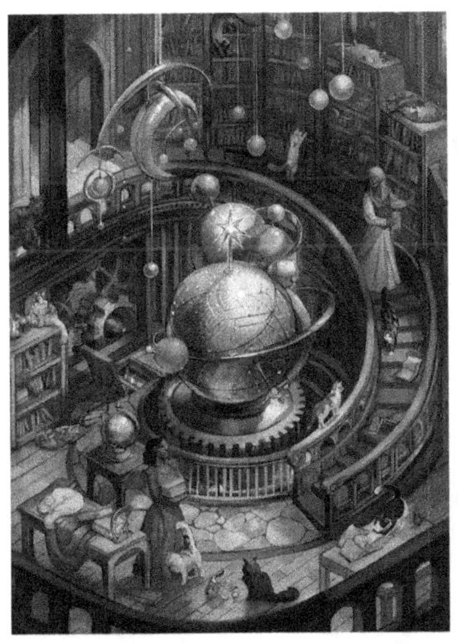

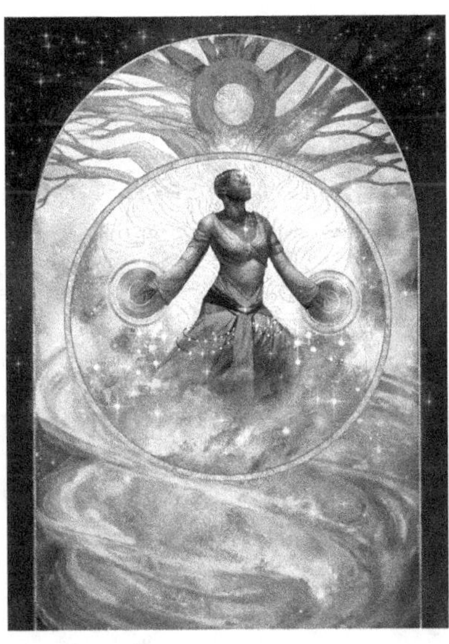

Scholars' Tower, personal work from *Imagined Realms: Book 1*
Cosmic Traveler, personal work from *Imagined Realms: Book 2: Earth and Sky*

Local Artist GoH: Tom Deadstuff

Ask Tom Deadstuff what he does and he'll suggest something overtly simple like, "I make stuff."

That's not just Tom being modest, though he is certainly his own worst critic; it's just that difficult to categorize his work, put it into a box and slap a label on it. Of course, if you literally put it into a box, he'd promptly turn that box into something else. It's what he does. Everything changes.

Ask his fans, who are legion, what he does and they'll flounder around trying to come up with a description too that goes beyond, "Well, it's Tom Deadstuff!" The man is his own genre. The best you're likely to get is that he makes things from other things using the art of paper mache.

Yes, paper mache. If you thought that the pinnacle of paper mache is what your neighbor's kid brings home from his fifth grade art class, boy, do you have a wake-up call coming! Tom's work is fine art and the price tags he unwillingly attaches to his work are only going to rise because the demand is already outstripping the supply. Come to think of it, exposing his talent to a regional audience at Westercon will only help that and so damage my intentions of buying a heck of a lot more than I already have.

The better half and I have been privileged to be able to watch Tom's work grow over a number of years and it's been a real treat.

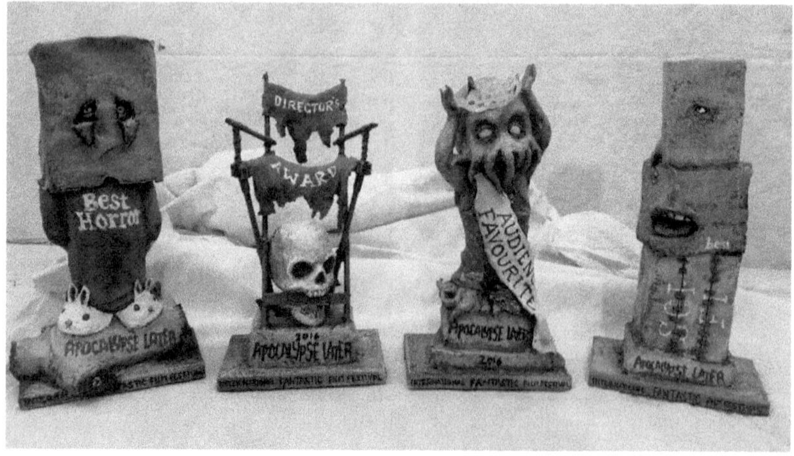

We first met him on Main Street in Mesa, during a Second Friday event, a monthly street fair that enlivens a sedate Mormon town with wild art and shenanigans. We were immediately struck by his imagination which, frankly, is not like anyone else's, not to mention his wry enthusiasm. We snapped up a few inexpensive pieces, demon babies and weirdly framed skeletons and the like, over a few Second Fridays.

When we wandered over to see his display at Phoenix FearCon de la Muertos, a fun local horror film festival and convention, in 2014, we were stunned to see much larger pieces: mermaids and other nautical creatures, some of which were five or six feet in height. Tom's art hadn't stood still since those Mesa days. It had grown and evolved.

When we heard that the Alwun House in Phoenix were going to host his first solo gallery exhibition in 2016, we were there with bells on. I found myself lost in half a dozen pieces, because there were layers now that I'd never seen before. Maybe it was the indoor lighting. Maybe it was more of that artistic evolution. One piece in particular watched me walk around the room, jealous of my examination of its peers. That piece now sits on our living room wall and watches everyone else who visits.

At this point, I already knew I wanted Tom to create the awards for my genre film festival. I provided him with a rough size and genre and let him run with it. My festival now has the best awards in the history of awards. The hardest thing I did last year was to post them to the winners.

What stuns me most is that even Tom doesn't know what his creations are going to be until they're partly done. With the inner vision of a true artist, he just somehow knows that this box here and those chopsticks and this stack of dog racing tickets and that roll of netting should go together and become... ah, it's a clownfish or a jackalope or a nightmare. I'll never stop wondering how he sees that, but hey, that's art.

I just know that, if I win the lottery, I'd hire Tom full time to make many more things and fill my house with them.

— Hal C. F. Astell

Director, Apocalypse Later International Fantastic Film Festival

Author GoH: Connie Willis

Connie Willis is kindly sponsored by the WesternSFA.

Many of you may know Connie Willis from her Oxford time travel stories, her holiday stories or her varied award winning short fiction. She is also well known within writer's circles as a good teacher, having done writing workshops many times over the years and helped numerous writers improve their craft. She has been recognized by fans and her peers many times with awards (Hugos, Nebulas, Locus and others) as well as having been honored by the Science Fiction and Fantasy Writers of America with the Damon Knight Memorial Grand Master Award.

It is fitting that Connie Willis is the Author Guest of Honor at a Westercon in Arizona. While she has spent most of her life in Colorado, she did live in the East part of the Phoenix metro area for a year or two that inspired the dystopian setting of the Hugo and Nebula award winning novella "The Last of the Winnebagos". While Van Buren didn't turn into a superhighway like in the novella (nor did all the dogs die), we do now have the 202 which runs just to the north of the Mission Palms.

Connie has been in Arizona several times before for conventions, including as Author Guest of Honor at CopperCon 23, Toastmaster at the 2006 Nebula Awards, and taking part at a LepreCon in Casa Grande with her daughter Cordelia, who was going to school at the University of Arizona at the time.

She is also a prime example of how the National Endowment for the Humanities (NEH) has contributed to the arts. Connie was able to launch her writing career due to a NEH Writer's Grant she received that allowed her to work full time and do the research that led to "Fire Watch", *Doomsday Book*, and the rest of the Oxford time travel series. Without that grant, Connie may have never gone on to have the success she did and pay it forward as she has been doing her entire career.

Connie is always happy to talk about many subjects including writing, politics, *Primeval* (especially *Primeval*), romantic comedies and much more.

So make sure you catch one or more of her panels this weekend and chat with her if you get a chance.

— Lee Whiteside

Chair, LepreCons 28, 36 and 37

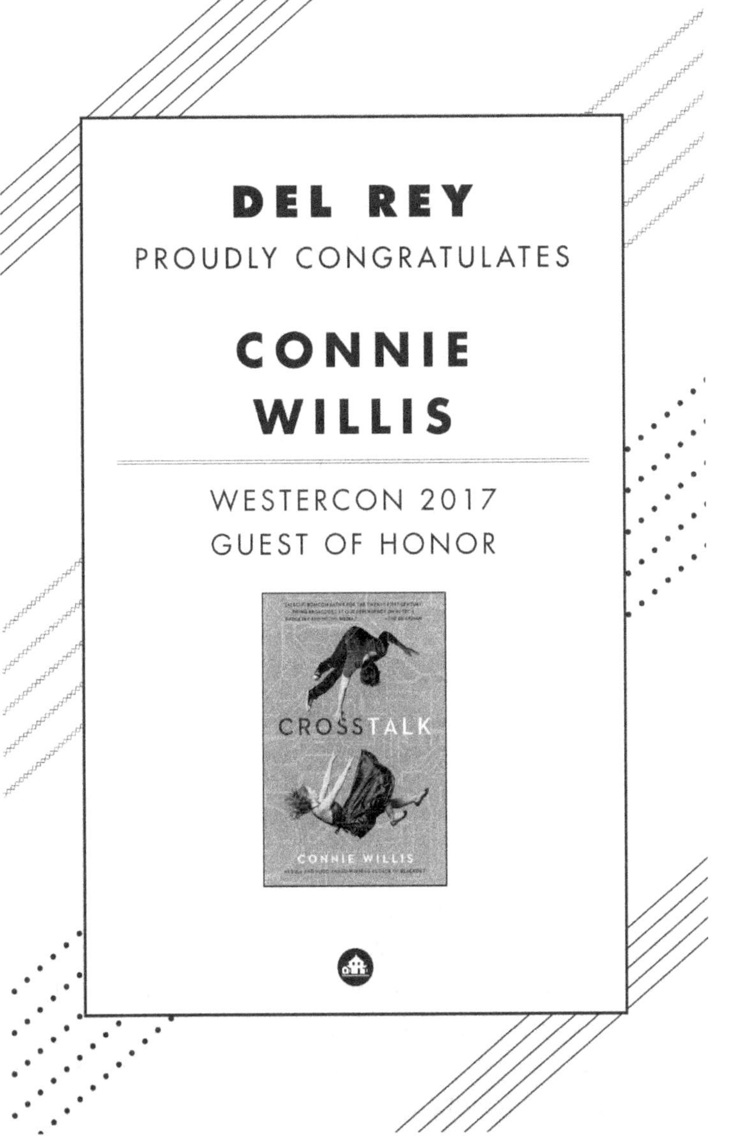

Local Author GoH: Gini Koch

Instantly recognizable by her sparkling pink cowboy hat and her loud, infectious laugh, most people know Gini Koch as the prolific author of the fast, fresh, and funny Alien/Katherine "Kitty" Katt series from DAW. But those of us from Arizona who are lucky enough to call her colleague, mentor, and/or friend know her as something more - we know her as a veritable force of (mostly benevolent) nature.

I first met Gini back in 2010 at CopperCon, when we were put together on a panel about religion and science fiction, largely because we were both editing genre ezines with a religious bent at the time. We emailed back and forth before the con and discovered we had a lot in common, including a sarcastic sense of humor that we wasted no time inflicting on each other. Then I showed up at the con and one of the first things Gini did was bring her entire entourage of fans (which she is rarely without at these events) to my reading and insist that they all buy my book.

That's how Gini is. When she takes you under her wing, she shares her 25+ years of marketing experience, her writing wisdom, her fan base, and, if you're a particular favorite, her love of teenage death ballads.

Gini was instrumental in getting me my first agent, invites to multiple anthologies, and introductions to a ton of people in the business. And I'm not unique. She goes out of her way to mentor other writers, both aspiring and more established, offering the benefits of her experience and contacts with a generous heart and a keen eye for talent she can help foster.

That's not to say she isn't harsh when she needs to be - no one benefits from an editor who won't say what has to be said - but it's always in service of the story, delivered in a way that shows her mentees what their strengths are while at the same time making sure they understand that this writing gig is not for the thin-skinned or the faint of heart.

She does all of this while maintaining a grueling schedule of at least two (very long) books a year, plus whatever short stories she might have in anthologies, plus the various signings, conventions, and book festivals she participates in throughout the year. Given all that, perhaps you can begin to understand that whole "force of nature" thing – she is a whirlwind, and to be caught up in her storm leaves you breathless and inspired, your heart beating faster as you ready yourself to take on the world, because she has made you believe you can.

Gini is not only an amazing writer in her own right, but she does her best to help other writers be amazing, too. That, to me, is the mark of a truly great author who deserves to be recognized. Westercon couldn't have chosen a better Local Author Guest of Honor. Well done!

— Marsheila Rockwell
author and poet

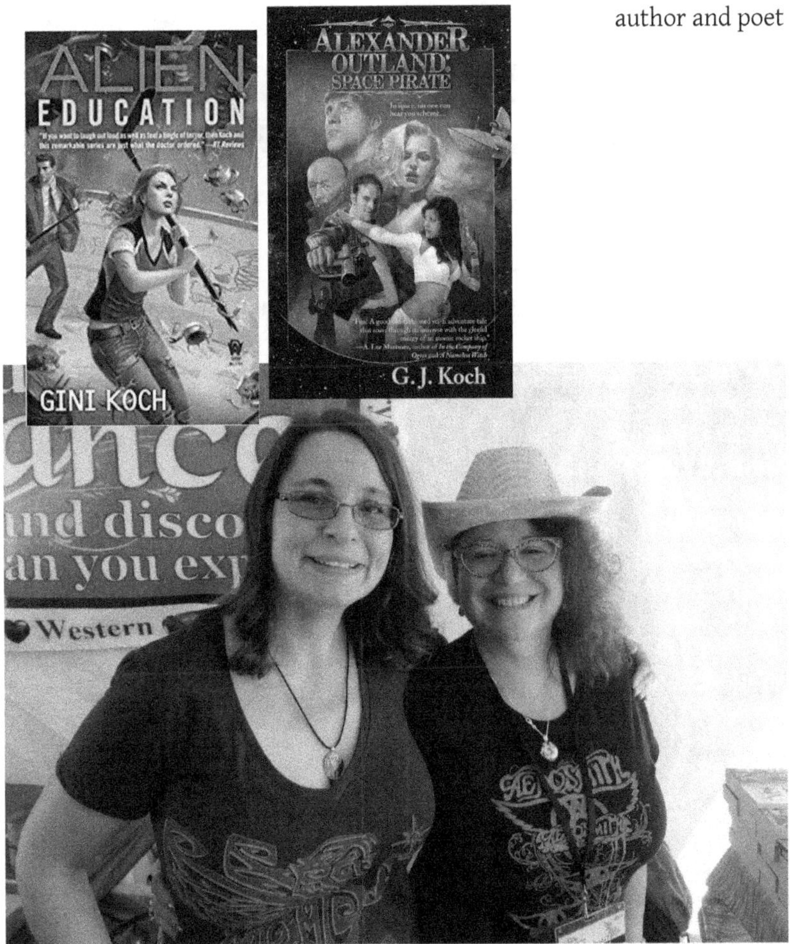

Fan GoHs: Val & Ron Ontell

Ron and Val Ontell have been involved in fandom since the 1960's. They are not content to sit on the sidelines and watch the show; they must be part of the magic.

As a librarian, Val has contacts in the publishing industry which allowed them to bring a book display and raffle to at least two World Science Fiction Conventions in Los Angeles, LACon III and LACon IV. Though the booth was staffed by convention gofers, both Ron and Val spent a lot of time there talking about books and authors and selling raffle tickets to everyone passing by.

As a travel agent, Ron has arranged foreign tours both before and after overseas Worldcons, which have included tea at the Ireland home of Anne McCaffrey and dinner at a restaurant with Dick Wolfe in Melbourne, Australia. Anyone who has been on one of their tours knows about the long days of touring as well as the incredible history found in each stop along the way. And, as everyone on the tours was gleaned from the Worldcon membership, we all had something in common to begin with and the friendships made are long lasting and memorable.

Because of their long years of meeting and greeting, the Ontells know personally many of the authors the rest of us have only met on the pages of their books. Though originally from New York, they've lived in San Diego for many years and helped establish two local conventions, ConDor and Conjecture, bringing writer guests from all over California and even further away to see and be seen. They have been an important part of backbone and guiding lights of these two conventions, acting as guest liaison, hotel liaison, registration, and any other position where a vacancy occurs. They have pulled their friends and neighbors along with them into the world of conventioning and of great science fiction and fantasy to help keep the fires of fandom burning.

Together and separately, they have worked more registration tables than would fit inside an average convention center and work tirelessly to help make any convention they're involved with an enjoyable experience for everyone, fans and guests alike.

Val has also been a panel participant, voicing her knowledge and opinions on all things literary. She was, in addition, chair of the World Fantasy convention in 2011, a job that has given her a great sense of accomplishment, so much so that she's looking forward to volunteering for that difficult job again in the not too distant future.

Their San Diego home is a tribute to their far-reaching interest in all things science fiction and fantasy with walls and walls of books covering the spectrum of the written word and beautiful art mostly acquired at convention art shows all over the world. Dragons are a special passion of Val's and appear in many of the pieces in all their forms.

— Steve & Katy Thorp

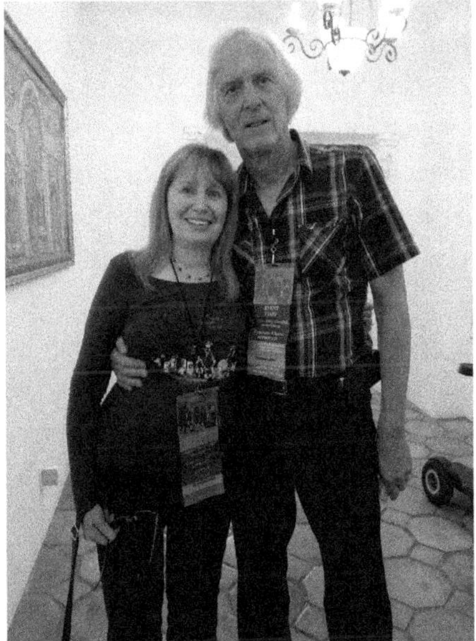

Filk GoH: Tim Griffin

Tim Griffin is kindly sponsored by the Phoenix Filk Circle.

The first time I heard Tim Griffin was at the 2011 Ohio Valley Filk Festival (OVFF) where he performed *Valent Shell* as his entry into the Ringmaster songwriting contest. He introduced himself as a former elementary school teacher and I remember leaning over to Bari and whispering "How come I never had teachers like him?" Tim's music, and the workshops he runs, are designed to make even complex subjects fun and accessible for kids of all ages through music, and his passion for this effervesces around him.

Since that first introduction in 2011, I have gotten to know Tim better and had many opportunities to share a circle with him, and I am always delighted when I can. My youngest son will grow up learning from his music, and both my adult children listen to his CDs. There is no age limit to enjoying his songs, and I have unabashedly learned many things I never did in school. In 2014, Tim very deservedly won the Pegasus Award for best songwriter-composer.

In a time when schools across the country are making harsh budget cuts, Tim is both a pioneer and evangelist for the importance of keeping art and music in schools, and how they enhance the learning of traditional academic subjects. Tim has been in the educational trenches, having taught for 18 years in Los Angeles, California Title-1 elementary schools. (Those are the schools with high numbers of disadvantaged students.) He has seen first hand how students retain information better when music is incorporated into the lessons, whether STEM, history or health.

Within fandom, he is an avid filk performer and supporter of the filk community, lending help wherever he can. I experienced his caring personally when, in 2014, I lost my music partner and husband, Bari. Though busy, Tim made a point to reach out to me in compassion, offering one of the most comforting emails I received and one I have saved to this day. He then graciously agreed to be my accompanist in 2015 for my first solo concert and we had a delightfully fun shared stage at the Spokane Worldcon.

When my daughter, Valerie, told me she wanted Tim as the Filk GoH for Westercon, I couldn't have been more pleased. I am also honored to have been asked to write an appreciation of Tim for the Program Book. I think Tim Griffin is one of the most important forces currently working for quality education, an exemplary filker and someone I am proud to call friend. Way to go, Tim!

— Cat Greenberg
filker

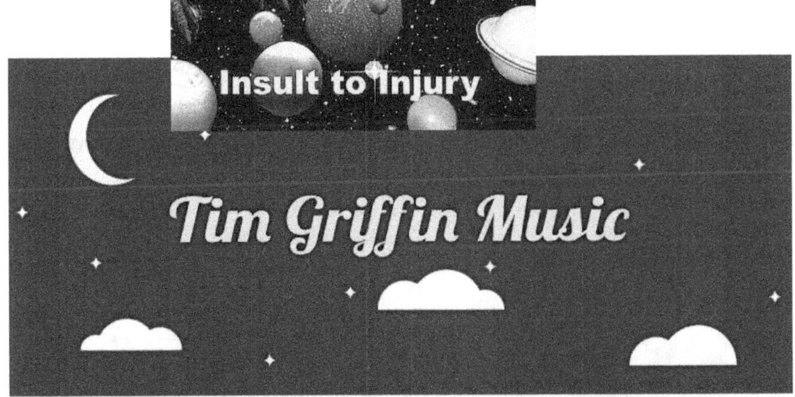

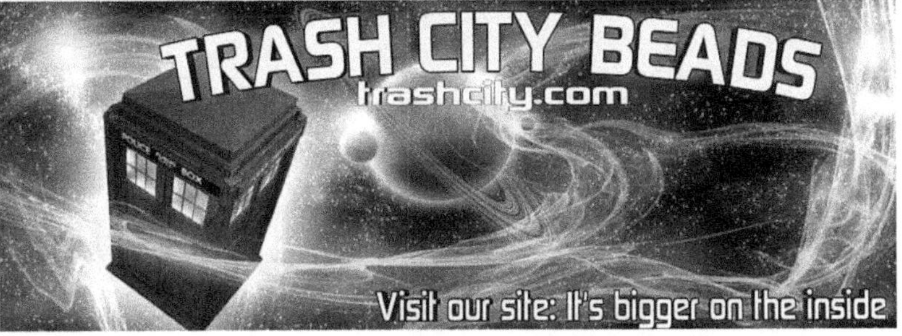

Science GoH: Henry Vanderbilt

I have watched Henry for many years as he created and ran the Space Access Conference. I firmly believe that the growth of the smaller space enterprises flourishing today owes much to Henry.

His major talent is understanding people. It showed in his early days in the L-5 Society, then in the Space Access Society, which he founded in 1992 and served as president until 2006. Later, he could gather fans and friends to staff Space Access. He could herd engineers and gather them into a cohesive group.

He is a wily conspirator. In 1994, he founded the Space Access aerospace engineering conference to lure in the small industry players so he could educate them in the fine arts of business and financial planning.

Though enormous technical advances resulted from the networking opportunities, the greater effect surely came from the financial, legal and government advisers who attended Space Access year on year. He had financiers, lawyers and government representatives from NASA and the FAA. They were often boring, but they were utterly necessary.

Henry's enthusiasm for space, plus his grit and determination, have put mankind a few important steps toward practical, low cost spaceflight. We owe him much.

— Gary Swaty

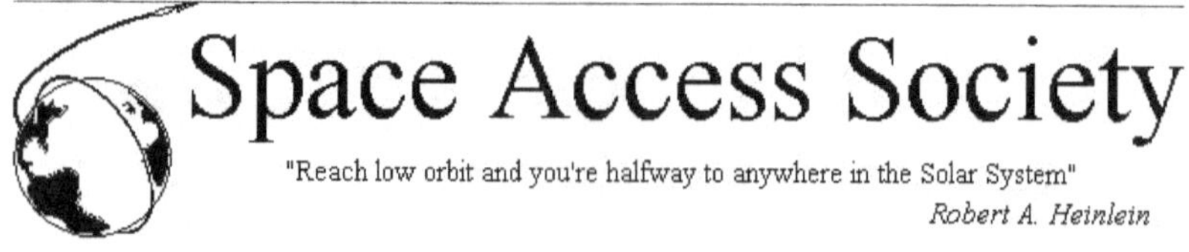

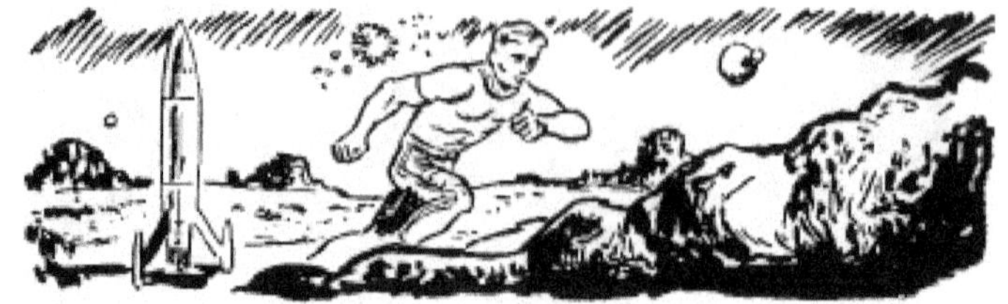

Special Artist GoH: Larry Elmore

Larry Elmore is kindly sponsored by LepreCon 44.

In some industries, there are legends who are larger than life and have withstood the test of time. For whatever reason, the public has decided that these few select individuals are the Elvises of their industry.

It is very rare when you get the chance to meet these legends, because most of them have passed away, but if you have the chance to meet a legend of the industry in an area you love, then jump on that chance. This year Westercon 70 has brought the Elvis of the gaming community to their convention. Of course I am speaking of Larry Elmore.

I first became acquainted with Elmore's work during the Christmas holiday season of 1989. I was a young impressionable kid in the 4th grade. I had just seen *Batman* earlier in the year; as a result I had picked up a pencil and started drawing on a regular basis. To further encourage my love for art my presents were mostly art related that year, including a collection of Burne Hogarth's *Dynamics* books, guides on Marvel and DC Comics, and collections of artwork from science fiction and fantasy artists.

My jaw dropped at some of the artwork I was seeing from Ken Kelly, Frank Frazetta, Neal Adams, and more. One of those pictures was *The Red Dragon* by Larry Elmore. I could not stop staring at that picture; the action, drama, suspense, and story being told in that one picture was just astounding. Elmore's style that day etched a permanent place in my brain.

The more time passed, the more I realized just how influential Elmore was. I would open up a brand new comic and there was an ad featuring Elmore's artwork. I would walk into a book store and see Elmore's work on gaming guides. I would go to the gaming store and again Elmore's artwork was everywhere to be seen. For a while, there just didn't seem like a place I could walk into and not see Elmore's work or the inspiration he gave others when they created their artwork.

Elmore had, in my eyes, taken the king's crown as the number one fantasy gaming artist in the industry. He had laid the groundwork and rules for his successors to follow with his *SnarfQuest* comic, cover art for *Dragonlance* books, early groundbreaking work for *Dungeons and Dragons*, and artwork for the *Magic: The Gathering* card game. He even indirectly set the standards for how many people think when creating characters for roleplaying games, as they imagine his artwork when doing so.

Almost 25 years has passed since Elmore became the king of the fantasy gaming world. I can't stress enough how rare it is to meet a talent of Elmore's level and status in the industry. If you are an aspiring artist, lover of fantasy artwork, gamer, or someone who just loves fantasy, then make sure to make all of Elmore's panels and stop by to visit him in the dealer's room. It's a chance to evolve your artistic styles, literary writing, and take a piece of Elmore's artwork home directly from the man himself.

— Michael Fett
Chair, LepreCon 44

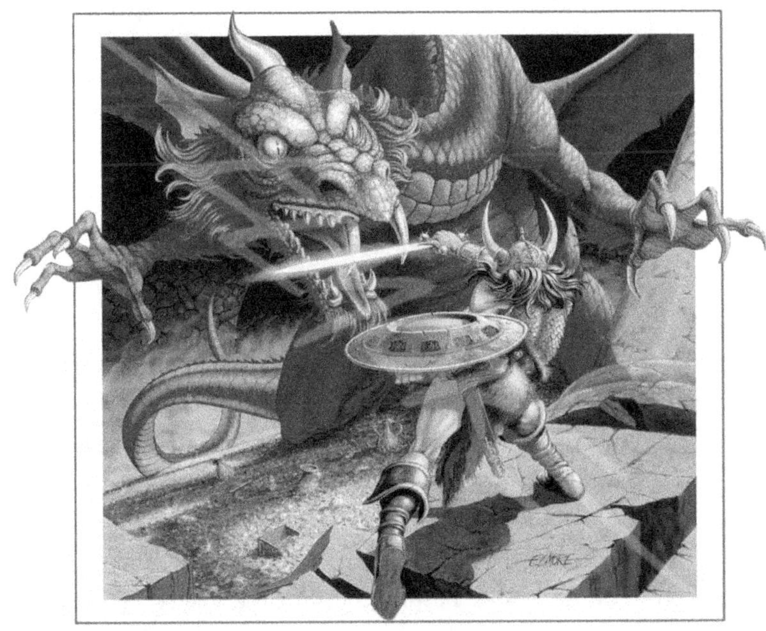

BASIC D&D THE RED DRAGON

Special Media GoHs: Bjo & John Trimble

Bjo & John Trimble are kindly sponsored in part by the United Federation of Phoenix.

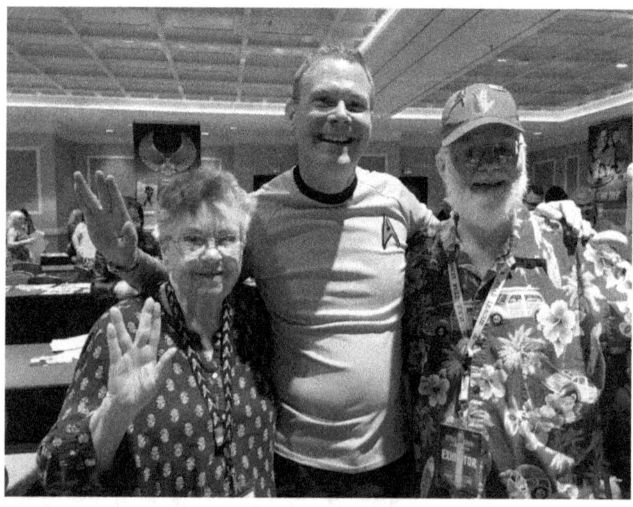

As president of the United Federation of Phoenix (Phoenix's oldest *Star Trek* fan club), it is my honor to welcome Bjo and John Trimble, the "Fans Who Saved *Star Trek*", to Westercon 70, as a part of the UFP's 50th Anniversary celebration of *Star Trek* (The Original Series)!

I met Bjo Trimble at a Save the Children charity fundraiser organized by the Far Beyond the Stars *Star Trek: Deep Space 9* actors fan club in Monrovia, CA back in 2004, but of course I knew about Bjo and her indefatigable husband John prior to that. It is part of *Star Trek* history how they organized and led a letter writing campaign to NBC Studios near the end of the second season of *TOS* in 1968 when the show was in danger of cancellation. Through their work, and the time and donations of many of the original *Trek* fans, over 1,000,000 letters were delivered to the NBC Studio offices in California and New York. This convinced NBC to renew the show for a third season. Despite the drop in quality in Season 3, enough episodes were produced (79) to sell the show into syndication in

1969, and *Star Trek* became known as "The Show That Wouldn't Die" throughout the 1970s. The show gained popularity, inspiring an animated series, a movie series, and 30 years ago, a sequel series *Star Trek: The Next Generation*, which itself inspired three additional sequel series, movies, not to mention books, games, merchandise, totaling over $## billion. Literally, all of *Star Trek* that's come since *TOS*, and all the subsequent science fiction TV shows developed based on the success of *TOS* and *TNG*, is due to the Trimbles. We all owe them a great debt of gratitude!

The Trimbles also spearheaded the letter writing campaign to President Ford to change the name of the first US space shuttle from Constitution to Enterprise, and Bjo was there for the roll out!

The Trimbles are no strangers to cons. As detailed in her 1983 memoir, *On the Good Ship Enterprise: My 15 Years with Star Trek*, Bjo describes how she ran the "Future Fashion Show" at the Cleveland Worldcon in 1966, including being asked to show off costumes from a new SF show that would be premiering in the fall, which the show's producer would screen there. That was how the Trimbles met Gene Roddenberry. *Star Trek* scripts were sold at Westercon 20 to support postage costs for the later 1968 letter writing campaign. The Trimbles and other *Star Trek* fans supported a raffle at Westercon 23 to help the American Cancer Society. At another Westercon they brought film strips from *TOS* episodes, which fans eagerly cut up and shared. And at Westercon 25 they and other *Trek* fans developed the idea of a west coast *Star Trek* convention, Equicon, which they helped run between 1973-1976. They have also been active in the SCA, the Los Angeles SF Society, the Planetary Society, the National Wildlife Fund, and the Smithsonian Institution. On top of that they had a family and raised two daughters!

We are truly honored to have Bjo and John Trimble join us for Westercon 70. Please visit them and make them feel welcome!

— David A. Williams, Ph.D.
Associate Research Professor, ASU School of Earth & Space Exploration
President, The United Federation of Phoenix

Toastmaster: Weston Ochse

About seventeen years ago, I met an affable, wholesome-looking fellow who was still in the early years of his writing career – no published novels, but a fair amount of short fiction, some of which had just been collected into a trade paperback. Expecting nothing more than a light-hearted read, I picked up a copy of *Scary Rednecks and Other Inbred Horrors...* and discovered that Weston Ochse is a much more complex individual and author than I had realized.

His accomplishments are wide-ranging and formidable. Weston is a father, the devoted husband of award-winning author Yvonne Navarro, an avid fan of Elvis Presley, and a gracious and generous host. He has rescued and raised Great Danes, successfully fly fished for salmon in Washington, and taught creative writing, advanced infantry, and military intelligence techniques. He has earned a Master of Fine Arts and authored some thirty books and a multitude of short stories and non-fiction articles for anthologies, literary journals, and magazines ranging from *Cemetery Dance* to *Soldier of Fortune*, including *Appalachian Galapagos* (Pushcart Prize

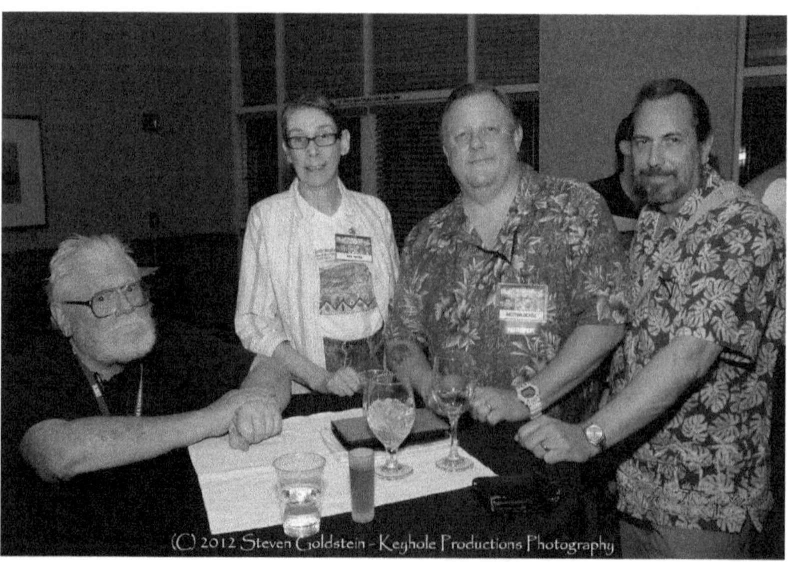

nominee), *Scarecrow Gods* (Bram Stoker Award for First Novel), *Redemption Roadshow* (Bram Stoker Award Finalist for Long Fiction), "The Crossing of Aldo Rey" (Bram Stoker Award Finalist for Short Fiction), *Multiplex Fandango* (Bram Stoker Award Finalist for Fiction Collection), "Righteous" (Bram Stoker Award Finalist for Short Fiction), *SEAL Team 666* (New Mexico-Arizona Book Award for Adventure or Drama Fiction), *Age of Blood* (New Mexico-Arizona Book Award for Science Fiction & Fantasy), *Reign of Evil* (New Mexico-Arizona Book Award for Adventure or Drama Fiction), and his *Task Force OMBRA* trilogy (*Grunt Life*, *Grunt Traitor*, and *Grunt Hero*), which directly confronts and explores post-traumatic stress disorder and the lives of PTSD survivors. He has thirty-five years (and counting) of service, first with Army Special Operations, then as an intelligence officer, and now with the Defense Intelligence Agency, which has led him to travel throughout the United States and to over fifty countries, including a six-month deployment to Kabul in 2013 and a dramatic four-hour layover in Dubai International Airport involving body armor, a stray round of ammunition, flashbacks from *Midnight Express*, and Bruce Lee.

In short, Weston is a chaotic good paladin who defies simple categorization or explanation. Weston Ochse's fiction – like Weston Ochse the man – is much the same.

Weston has an intense and thoughtful awareness of the passion, joy, capriciousness, and absurdity of the human condition, together with the insight, craft, and talent to turn those observations into a powerful, compelling, and captivating tale. Weston has the skill to evoke laughter, tears, and terror as he probes and lays bare the darkness within his characters and the worlds they inhabit, often revealing unexpected strength, nobility, and heroism from the unlikeliest sources. Weston's fiction has been described as many things; "boring" and "predictable" are not among them. Nor, I suspect, will those words apply to his role as Toastmaster for this year's Westercon.

— Kevin McAlonan
Treasurer, Westercon 70
Secretary, Leprecon, Inc.

Convention Policies

Westercon 70 is sponsored by Leprecon, Inc. so we've adopted their standard set of policies for our event.

Anti-Harassment Policy

Westercon 70 wishes to provide a safe, hospitable, harassment-free convention experience for everyone, regardless of gender, gender identity, gender expression, sexual orientation, marital status, physical or mental ability or disability, physical appearance, coloration, physical attributes, age, body size, body shape, race, ethnicity, citizenship status, employment, socioeconomic status, financial status, familial status, military or veteran status, achievements, national origin, ancestry, worldview, political party preference, political belief, political affiliation, operating systems, platform preference, programming language, text editor preference, creed or religion (or lack thereof).

The purpose of this policy is to deter and address harassment and harmful conduct, not to limit consensual interaction and free and open discussion.

We expect all attendees, participants, guests, members, volunteers, and staff to act responsibly, courteously, and considerately, and to follow this code of conduct during all conventions, convention-related events, and convention meetings.

"Yes" means yes, "no" means no, and "maybe" means no. Please take "no" for an answer for any request or activity and do not repeat your request again. Do not corner people socially; if someone is looking apprehensive or trapped, give them space. If someone tells you to go away or to leave him or her alone, your business with that person is done and you should not attempt to initiate further contact with that person.

No touching or photographing other people without consent. This includes glomping, hugging, kissing, fondling, hands on knees, backs, shoulders, and hair - just ask first! The fact that someone is in costume does not imply consent for photographs or touching - again, ask first!

Obtain permission before posting images of people or recordings of the convention online. Do not assume that physical contact will be welcome or appreciated. Some do not like to be touched and will respect and like you more if you respect their personal space. You are encouraged to ask for unequivocal consent for all activities.

Westercon 70 welcomes families with children and expects all attendees, participants, guests, members, and staff to treat these families with courtesy. Use of explicit sexual language and imagery should be limited to panels, events, and situations where those in attendance know that such content may be presented. Parents or guardians should be aware not all panels or events may be suitable for children. Parents or guardians bringing children are responsible for their children's behavior.

Westercon 70 does not tolerate harmful conduct or harassment of or by attendees, participants, guests, members, volunteers and staff in any form. Harmful conduct or harassment is verbal or physical conduct that creates an unpleasant or hostile situation. This includes, but is not limited to:

1. Physical assault.
2. Battery.
3. Disregarding the safety of other persons.
4. Theft or robbery.
5. Intentional destruction of property.
6. Deliberate intimidation.
7. Stalking.
8. Deliberate impeding or blocking another's movement.
9. Sexual attention, gestures, questions or comments that are known or ought reasonably to be known to be unwelcome.
10. Sexual advances or propositions that are known or ought reasonably to be known to be unwelcome.
11. Sexual advances or propositions toward a person under the age of eighteen.
12. Making or threatening reprisals after receiving a negative response to sexual advances or propositions.
13. Inappropriate and non-consensual physical contact, including

pinching, grabbing, patting, groping, or brushing against another's body.

14. Repeated heckling, interruption or other disruption of panels or other events or meetings.
15. Photography, audio or video recording without the subject's consent.
16. Posting images or content on the internet, Facebook, or other media without the consent of the subject of the image or content, or not removing images or content you have been asked to take down by the subject of the image or content.
17. Providing or offering to provide alcoholic beverages or illegal substances to someone under the age of 21.
18. Threatening, bullying, hectoring, coercion or any other abusive conduct that has the purpose or effect of unreasonably interfering with another person's ability to enjoy and participate in the convention, convention related events and convention meetings.
19. Inappropriate verbal comments or gestures related to gender, gender identity, gender expression, sexual orientation, marital status, physical or mental ability or disability, physical appearance, coloration, physical attributes, age, body size, body shape, race, ethnicity, citizenship status, employment, socioeconomic status, financial status, familial status, military or veteran status, achievements, national origin, ancestry, worldview, political party preference, political belief, political affiliation, operating systems, platform preference, programming language, text editor preference, creed or religion (or lack thereof).
20. Falsely accusing an innocent person of harassment.
21. Any other action or behavior that causes significant interference with convention operations, adversely affects the convention's relationship with its venues or the public, or causes excessive discomfort to other attendees, participants, guests, members, volunteers or staff.

Reasonable and objective examination of beliefs, including critical commentary on another person's views, does not by itself constitute harassment. One of the underlying rationales of this policy is to promote - not inhibit - discussion and free exchanges of ideas between persons of differing views. Furthermore, the responsibility for settling interpersonal disputes lies solely with the individuals involved, and Westercon 70 will not tolerate being used as a leveraging point in such disputes.

Persons asked to stop any harmful conduct or harassing behavior are expected to comply immediately. The exact remedy for harmful conduct or harassing conduct will depend on an evaluation of all relevant circumstances, such as the severity of the conduct and prior violations by the person engaging in prohibited conduct. Anyone violating this policy may be expelled from the meeting, event, or convention without a refund at the discretion of the convention organizers. Sanctions may include permanent suspension of membership of any future Leprecon Inc. events. When there is a reasonable basis for believing the conduct is illegal, appropriate law enforcement authorities will be notified.

If you are being harassed, notice that someone else is being harassed or engaging in harmful conduct, or have any other concerns, please contact a member of convention staff immediately. Convention staff can be identified by special badges.

Where convention staff witnesses to the prohibited conduct, immediate remedial action may be taken. Where a report of harmful conduct or harassment is made to convention staff after the conduct has occurred, reasonable measures will be taken to establish the facts. This will typically include discussion with witnesses, if any, and the person accused of engaging in the prohibited conduct. Inquiries into harmful conduct or harassing conduct will be carried out as confidentially as possible given the circumstances.

Convention staff will be happy to help participants contact hotel/venue security or local law enforcement, provide escorts, or otherwise assist those experiencing harassment to feel safe for the duration of the convention. We truly value your attendance and are here to help.

Photography and Videography

There is to be no photographic or videographic recording of individuals without explicit consent. The fact that someone is in costume does not imply consent for photos or videos – please just ask first! Always obtain permission before posting images or recordings of people online. Program Participants and Guests of Honor may or may not allow recording of their likeness or voice. You are encouraged to ask for unequivocal consent for all activities. If someone does not consent, fully respect their decision.

Weapons and Cosplay

The carrying and wearing of weapons must explicitly be for the use for cosplaying. All weapons and any props deemed possibly dangerous (ex. sharp edges or an item that could be used as a blunt object) must be inspected and peace-bonded by security staff. No real firearms are allowed, nor any firearms that could be easily mistaken for a real one. Bladed weapons are allowed but must be sheathed at all times.

Any weapons purchased in the Vendor Hall must be securely wrapped before they are taken out of the room.

The safety of convention members is our overriding consideration, as well as cooperating fully with the hotel's security personnel and their own weapons policy. Westercon 70 is a family event in a public venue, so we ask that you please be modest in your costume attire.

Fan Tables

Fan Tables are complimentary for non-profits and community outreach organizations. If an individual wishes to sell items for purely a profit venture, then they must be in the Merchant Hall. However, if a convention or fan group wants to sell memberships or merchandise to raise funds to help their parent organization, then this is both allowed and encouraged.

Fan Table Coordinators must purchase at minimum an Attending Full Membership. Any others staffing that Fan Table are encouraged, but not required, to purchase their own memberships. A Fan Table is defined as above; anything outside this definition requires a Vendor Table or Promotional Booth.

Room Parties

Room Party Coordinators must purchase at minimum an Attending Full Membership. Others who are either staffing or attending a party are encouraged – but not required – to purchase their own memberships. Room Party Coordinators are allowed to book a room/suite for a party at the convention rate. They will be located in the party area, and they must conform to any convention-specific party rules and regulations as specified by the convention chair and/or committee.

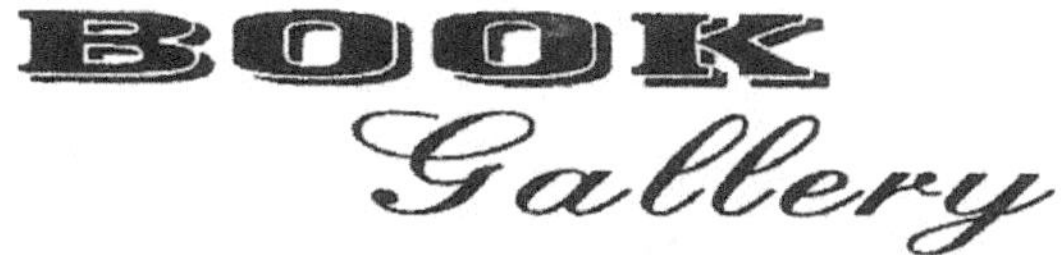

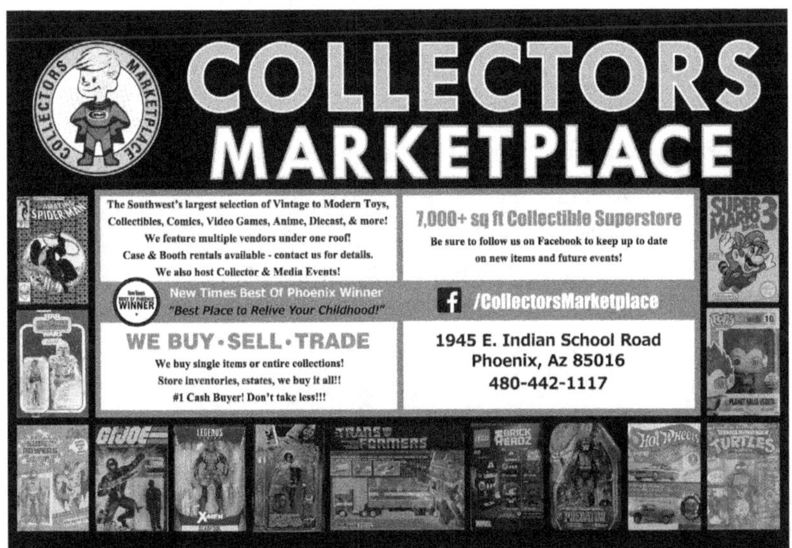

Art Show

Art Shows are a tradition at most sci-fi conventions, but they've been a special focus at LepreCon since the one that didn't happen, LepreCon VI in 1980. Canceled three weeks out because of issues with the hotel, a hastily organized fan gathering, AlterCon, replaced it, at which $1,700 of art was sold, even with an attendance of only 100.

As Terry Gish wrote in her retrospective in the LepreCon 11 program book, "Phoenix fans had demonstrated an appreciation for fine S/F art." So the planners of LepreCon VII, at which $4,000 of art was sold, set the stage for the succeeding decades in Phoenix fandom: LepreCon focuses on art, while CopperCon focuses on literature.

Hours

Our Art Show is being held in Palm B and C, which can be accessed via the Dealers' Room. Everything Art Show related will be in the Art Show, including the Artists' Reception on Sunday evening, except for the Art Auction for items with three or more written bids.

The Art Auction will be in the Cloister, after the Charity Auction.

Scheduled hours are:

Art Show (Palm B and C)

Friday	3.00pm - 9.00pm	Staff Set-Up
Saturday	10.00am - 1.00pm	Artist Check-In
	3.00pm - 7.00pm	Open to Members
Sunday	10.00am - 7.00pm	Open to Members
	5.00pm - 7.00pm	Artists' Reception
Monday	10.00am - 2.00pm	Open to Members
	4.00pm - 6.00pm	Artist Pick-Up
Tuesday		Art Show Closed

Cloister

Monday	4.00pm - 5.30pm	Auction
	5.30pm - 6.00pm	Auction Close-Out

Westercon 70 Artists

Here are the artists displaying in the Art Show at Westercon 70:

Ruth Merrill Bollerud	
Michael Brugger	grillghod.daportfolio.com
Manny Burruel	mannysartgallery.com
Sarah Clemens	clemensart.com
Daniel Cortopassi	danielcortopassi.com
Tom Cox	
Julie Dillon	juliedillonart.com
Branden Duncan	clockworkart.com
Gilead	fantasyartbygilead.com
Larry Gomez	larrygomez.com
Tabitha Ladin	tabithaladin.com
Lubov	lubov.net
Theresa Mather	rockfeatherscissors.com
Brigid Nelson	etsy.com/shop/hernecessarybaggage
David Lee Pancake	davidleepancake.com
Catherine Roop	catherineroop.com
Karen Roop	aliensoflactopia.com
Bjo Trimble	ancientearthpigments.com
Ralph J. Ryan	skyships1.com
Julie Verley	diranda.com
Bryan L. Wickham	facebook.com/offhandgallery
Mark Wickham	facebook.com/offhandgallery
S. L. Wickham	facebook.com/offhandgallery

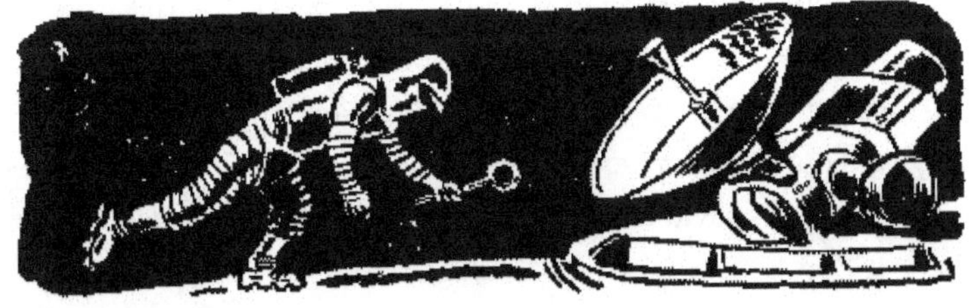

Author Events

In addition to the many panels and workshops in our Books and Authors track, we're also scheduling readings and autograph sessions. Our three author Guests of Honor will each have a dedicated meet and greet. We'd have scheduled kaffeeklatsches too, but hotel restrictions mean that they would be sans kaffee, so, in a way, we just have klatches.

Schedules may be subject to change (or additions!), so check signage for the latest version.

Meet and Greets

All our meet and greets will be in the Boardroom and will run for an hour.

Sunday	11.00am	**Weston Ochse**
Monday	3:30pm	**Connie Willis**
Tuesday	12:30pm	**Gini Koch**

Readings

All our readings will be in the Boardroom and will run for an hour.

Saturday	12.30pm	Linda D. Addison, Colette Black, Maya Bohnhoff
	2.00pm	Ashley Carlson, Jenn Czep, Emily Devenport, Stephanie Weippert
	3.30pm	Connie Cookrell, Ryan Dalton, J. L. Doty
Sunday	2.00pm	J. L. Doty, Janie Franz, Ernest Hogan
	3.30pm	Sandra Greenberg, H. Paul Honsinger, Eric T. Knight
Monday	9.30am	Michael D'Ambrosio, Suzanne Lazear, Jacqueline Lichtenberg
	12.30pm	Syd Logsdon, Yvonne Navarro, T. L. Smith
	2.00pm	Tom Leveen, Jeff Mariotte, Sharon Skinner
	5.00pm	Amy K. Nichols, Jamie Wyman, Natalie Wright
Tuesday	2.00pm	Deena Remiel, Frankie Robertson, Marsheila Rockwell
	3.30pm	David Lee Summers, Cynthia Ward, Thomas Watson

Autograph Schedule

All our autograph sessions will be in the Cloister and will run for an hour. Monday sessions are restricted to allow for the Charity and Art Auctions.

Saturday	2.00pm	Linda D. Addison, Colette Black, Maya Bohnhoff, Ryan Dalton, J. L. Doty, Jamie Wyman
	3.30pm	Ashley Carlson, Bruce Davis, Syd Logsdon, Amy K. Nichols, T. L. Smith, Stephanie Weippert
Sunday	11.00am	Connie Cookrell, Ryan Dalton, J. L. Doty, H. Paul Honsinger, Jacqueline Lichtenberg, **Bjo & John Trimble**
	12.30pm	Jenn Czep, T. L. Smith, David Lee Summers, Thomas Watson, Natalie Wright
	2.00pm	Emily Devenport, Tom Leveen, Jeff Mariotte, Yvonne Navarro, Marsheila Rockwell, **Connie Willis**
	3.30pm	**Julie Dillon**, Janie Franz, Amy K. Nichols, Deena Remiel, Frankie Robertson, Jamie Wyman
	5.00pm	Ernest Hogan, Eric T. Knight, **Weston Ochse**
Monday	11.00am	Linda D. Addison, Colette Black, Connie Cookrell, Michael D'Ambrosio, Frankie Robertson, Cynthia Ward
Tuesday	11.00am	Michael D'Ambrosio, T. L. Smith, David Lee Summers, Thomas Watson, Stephanie Weippert, **Connie Willis**
	12.30pm	Hal C. F. Astell, Bruce Davis, J. L. Doty, H. Paul Honsinger, Suzanne Lazear, Syd Logsdon
	2.00pm	Linda D. Addison, Emily Devenport, Janie Franz, Yvonne Navarro, Amy K. Nichols, Deena Remiel
	3.30pm	**Gini Koch**, **Weston Ochse**, Frankie Robertson

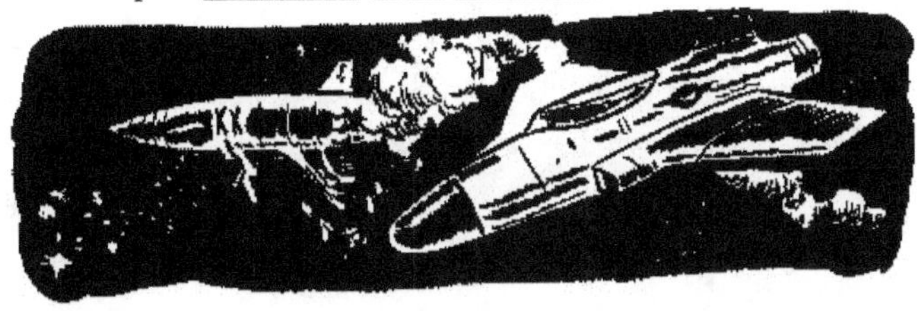

Charity Auction

Our Charity auction is scheduled for Monday at 1.30pm in the Cloister.

Charity

This auction will benefit the Challenger Space Center in Peoria, AZ, a 501(c)(3) non-profit institution that provides programs to help children understand the importance of math, science and technology along with teamwork, problem-solving, leadership and decision-making. Their high-tech, high-touch programs are molding the community and workforce leaders of the future.

Donations are vital to keep these programs available.

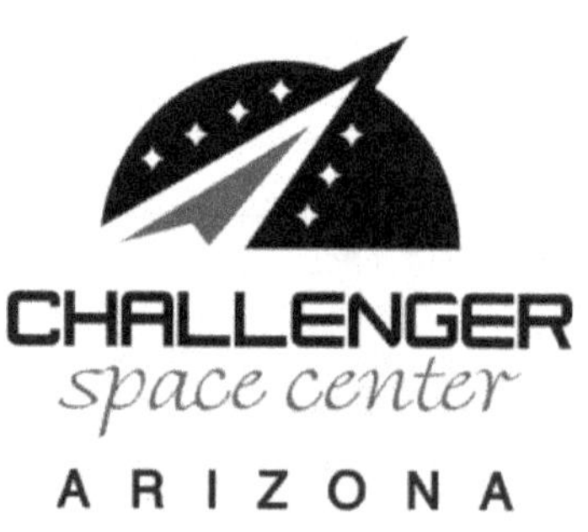

We guarantee everyone who shows up will have a good time and plenty of opportunity to bid on and take home cool stuff. We'll have books galore, space and science items, fantasy art, collectible art, and lots of film memorabilia. Everything will be on display in the Art Show until the auction begins.

Program Guides

There will be Charity Auction Program Guides available at Registration, listing all items under the hammer.

Research Before Bidding

Always inspect items prior to the Auction. They will be on display in the Art Show over the weekend.

All books that are presented as a First Edition are done so at the best judgment of our Charity Auction Director. No guarantee is made by Westercon 70 for any item. Thanks and happy bidding!

— Catherine Book
Charity Auction Director

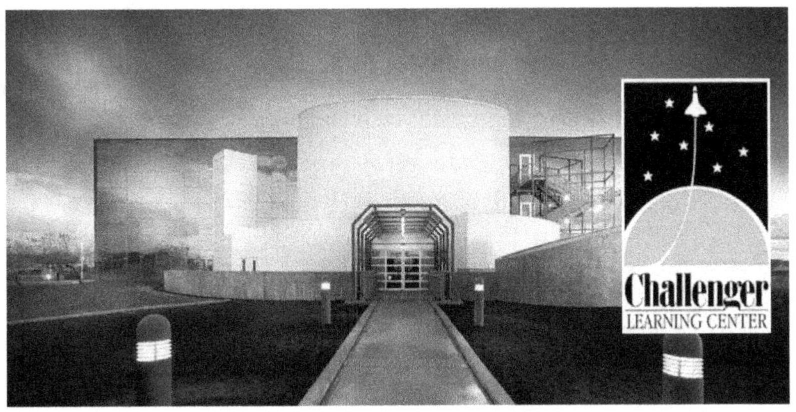

Westercon 70 would like to thank the generous donators to our auction:

Arizona Penny Dreadfuls	azpennydreadfuls.org
Book Gallery	bookgallery.com
Sarah Clemens	clemensart.com
Collectors' Marketplace	collectorsmarketplace.com
Ron Collins	typosphere.com
DAW Books	penguin.com/publishers/daw
J. L. Doty	jldoty.com
Drawn to Comics	drawntocomics.com
Imperial Outpost Games	imperialoutpostgames.com
Leprecon, Inc.	leprecon.org/corp
Tom Leveen	tomleveen.com
Jacqueline Lichtenberg	simegen.com/jl
Jeff Mariotte	jeffmariotte.com
Marsheila Rockwell	marsheilarockwell.com
Samurai Comics	samuraicomics.com
David Lee Summers	zianet.com/dsummers
Trash City Beads	trashcity.com
Trash City Film	trashcityentertainment.com
Bjo Trimble	facebook.com/thetrimbles
Thomas Watson	facebook.com/thomas.watson
Dr. David Williams	sese.asu.edu

Dealers' Room

Here are the Merchants who you'll find in our Dealers' Room. Please show your appreciation by buying their goods.

Amazing Wyked Writers	tlsmithbooks.com
Baron's Beauties	baronsbeauties.com
Book Universe, Inc.	facebook.com/bookuniverseinc
Michael Bradley Books	mbtimetraveler.com
Cargo Cult Books & Notions	abebooks.com/cargo-cult-books-notions-berkeley-ca/
The Worlds of Michael D'Ambrosio	fracturedtime.com
Tom Deadstuff	tomdeadstuff.com
Duncan's Books and More	duncansbooksandmore.com
Larry Elmore	larryelmore.com
Tim Griffin	griffined.org
Hip Pocket Creations	facebook.com/hippocketcreations
Jean's Beads	jeansbeads.com
Gini Koch	ginikoch.com
Left Hand Asylum	lefthandasylum.etsy.com
Little Bit of Everything (Sue Martin)	
Massoglia Books	alibris.com/stores/martysbooks
Model Building Secrets	
Moebius Enterprises	moebiusenterprises.com
Mystic Publishers Inc.	mysticpublishersinc.com
October Art	octoberart.com
Portico Arts	archwayportico.com
Vixen's Cosplay Closet Boutique	facebook.com/cosplayclosetboutique
Weegonza Bazaar	weegonza.com

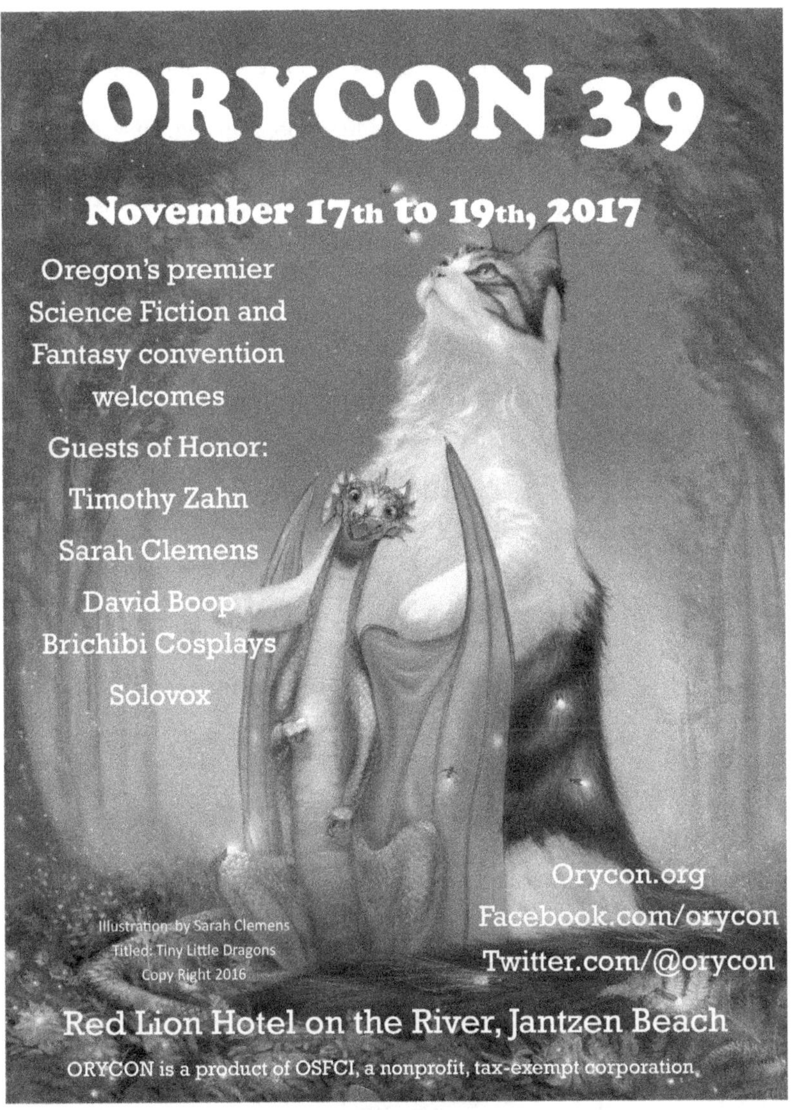
ORYCON 39
November 17th to 19th, 2017
Oregon's premier
Science Fiction and
Fantasy convention
welcomes
Guests of Honor:
Timothy Zahn
Sarah Clemens
David Boop
Brichibi Cosplays
Solovox
Orycon.org
Facebook.com/orycon
Twitter.com/@orycon
Illustration by Sarah Clemens
Titled: Tiny Little Dragons
Copy Right 2016
Red Lion Hotel on the River, Jantzen Beach
ORYCON is a product of OSFCI, a nonprofit, tax-exempt corporation.

Fan Tables

Our Fan Tables are located in the foyer outside the Palm Ballroom.

Blue Ribbon Army	blueribbonarmy.wildapricot.org
Costume-Con 36	cc36sandiego.org
Desert Brick	facebook.com/desertbrick
The DREAD Fleet	thedreadfleet.com
Operation Supply Drops Team	operationsupplydrop.org
Other Worlds Alliance	facebook.com/otherworldsalliance
Phoenix Astronomical Society	pasaz.org
Royal Manticoran Navy	trmn.org
Utah for 2019 Westercon Bid	utahfor2019.com
WorldCon 76	worldcon76.org

Len Berger will maintain a table for freebies in this area and provide free movie posters on tables just around the side of the Palm Ballroom. Just follow the sign!

Please leave your business cards, flyers, bookmarks and whatnot on the freebie table; and take movie posters (one per title per person, please).

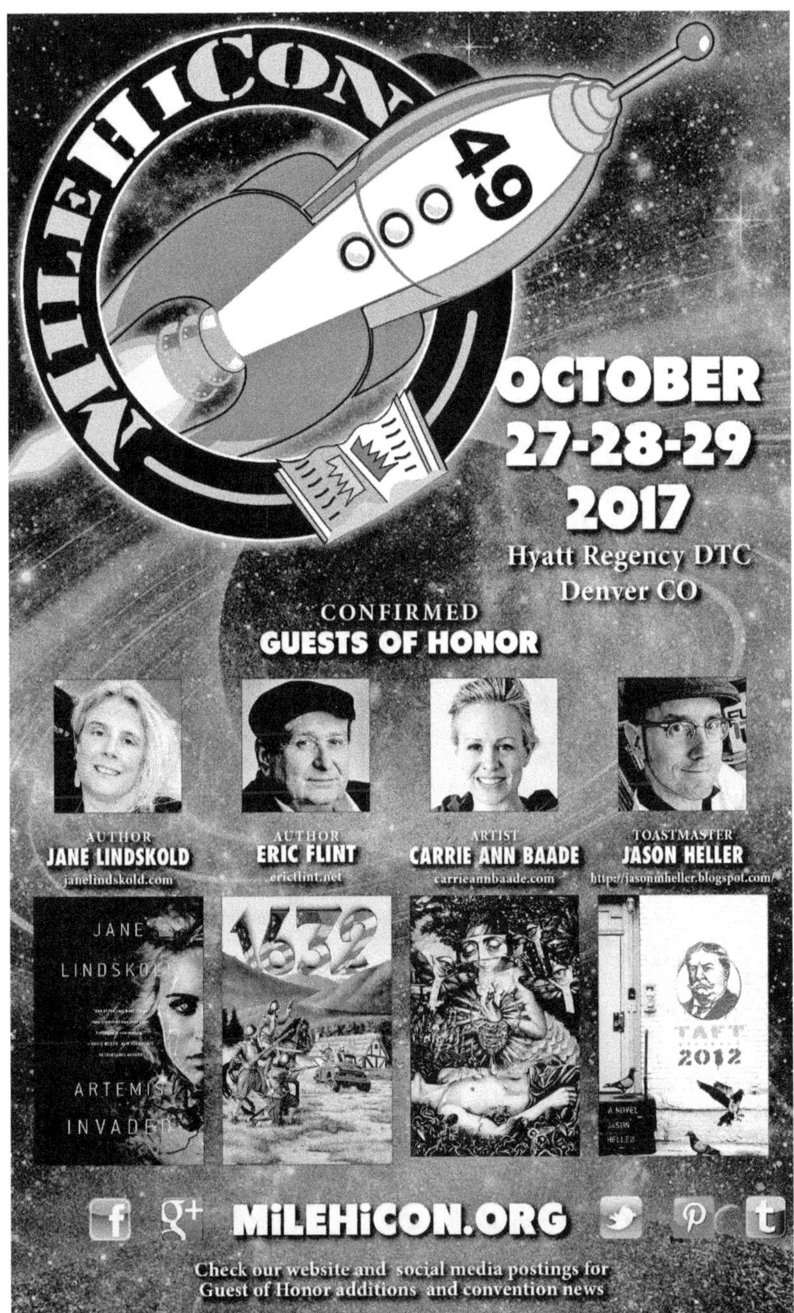
MiLEHiCON
49
OCTOBER
27-28-29
2017
Hyatt Regency DTC
Denver CO
CONFIRMED
GUESTS OF HONOR
AUTHOR
JANE LINDSKOLD
janelindskold.com
AUTHOR
ERIC FLINT
ericflint.net
ARTIST
CARRIE ANN BAADE
carrieannbaade.com
TOASTMASTER
JASON HELLER
http://jasonmheller.blogspot.com/
JANE
LINDSKOLD
ARTEMIS
INVADED
1632
TAFT
2012
A NOVEL
JASON
HELLER
MiLEHiCON.ORG
Check our website and social media postings for
Guest of Honor additions and convention news

Film Festival

Schedule

Our Film Festival will take place in the Wind Flower room, which is on the first floor, at the opposite end of the hallway from the ConSuite.

Sets are scheduled as follows:

Saturday	10.00am	Comic Book Films
	12.00pm	Fantasy Films Block 1
	2.00pm	Fantasy Films Block 2
	4.00pm	Horror Films
	6.00pm	Sci-Fi Films Block 1
Sunday	10.00am	Sci-Fi Films Block 2
	12.00pm	Sci-Fi Films Block 3
	2.00pm	Comic Book Films
	4.00pm	Fantasy Films Block 1
	6.00pm	Fantasy Films Block 2
Monday	10.00am	Horror Films
	12.00pm	Sci-Fi Films Block 1
	2.00pm	Sci-Fi Films Block 2
	4.00pm	Sci-Fi Films Block 3
	6.00pm	Award Ceremony

Comic Book Films

MERCS (UK, 40m, dir: Michael Morris)

A graphic novel stylized action film set in a hyper reality world where soldiers for hire clash and bullets fly. A mix of live action and animation bring this classic tale to life.

Heroes Manufactured (Canada, 70m, dir: Yaron Betan)

A documentary about Canadian independent comic artists trying to break into the industry while facing pop culture's biggest challenges. We explore the reality of producing superheroes in a market saturated with artists, writers, celebrities, cosplayers and everything else the comic-con markets have to offer. While it is set in Canada, the film explores a variety of independent artists that show the importance of their work through multiculturalism and their gender. *Heroes Manufactured* highlights artists from a variety of backgrounds including Mexican, Jewish, feminist and French-Canadian.

Fantasy Films Block 1

Song of the Starslayer: Part 1 (USA, 120m, dir: Robert M. Towne)

For centuries the Kingdom of Ashelon has toiled under the yolk of the Dragon, but not all will bow to the will of their Draconian overlords. An ancient order of knights devoted to resisting the might of Draconia has established a stronghold in the mountain halls of Fellcroft, and now wages war against the Dragon's empire. In the midst of this struggle, one dishonored knight seeks to restore his fortunes whilst winning the hand of the king's daughter in marriage. But this restless soul will soon find himself on a quest that will test his loyalties and decide the fate of the empire for good or ill.

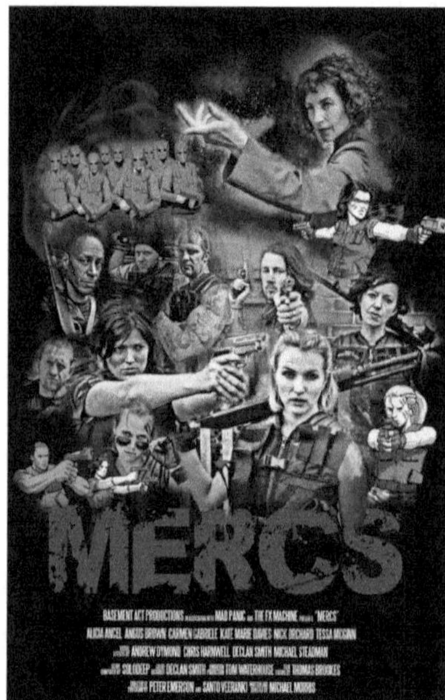

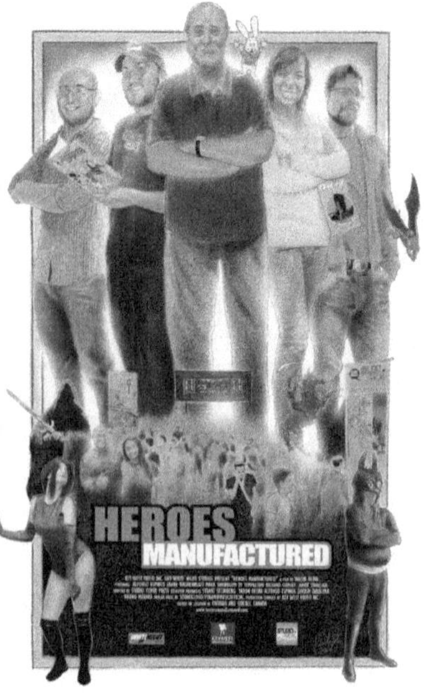

Fantasy Films Block 2

Song of the Starslayer: Part 2 (USA, 68m, dir: Robert M. Towne)

See above.

Lady Lillian (USA, 8m, dir: Danger Vision)

A dark comedy about a tarot reader/psychic whose rambling and somewhat absurd conversations with clients become self-fulfilling prophesies.

Horror Films

Prairie Dog (Canada, 94m, dir: Blake Evernden)

A lone sheriff in the vast lands and valleys of Brada County is confronted with a dual mystery. A pair of sociopathic criminals being chased across the plains have disappeared, and reports keep surfacing of a large, shadowed animal roaming the farmlands of the county. With the assistance of an environmental consultant and the mayor of the nearby town of Sombra Hollow, the sheriff races to find the connection between the mysteries that haunt the valleys of Brada County.

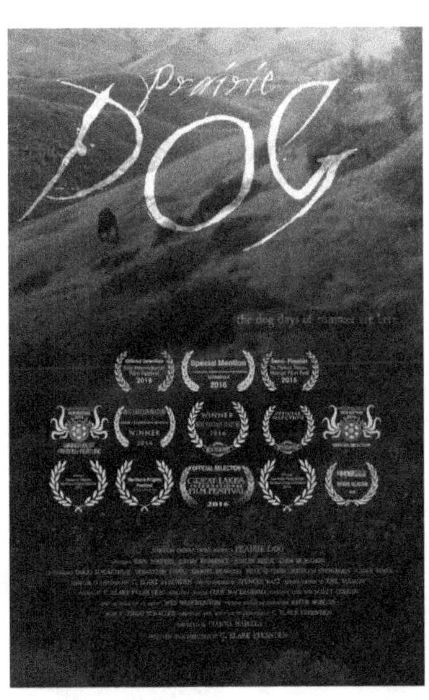

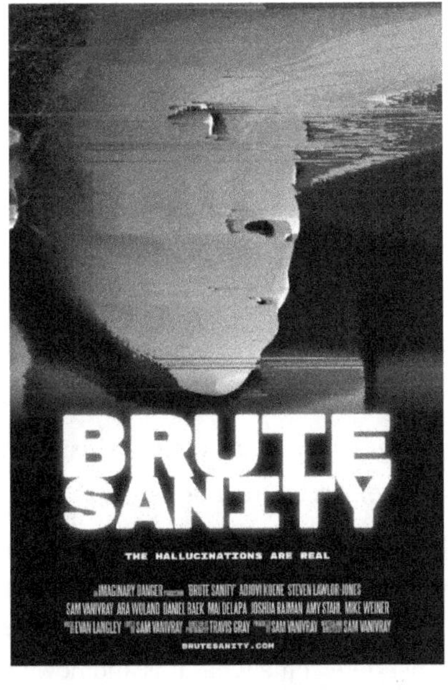

SONG OF THE STARSLAYER

Mr. Dentonn (Spain, 9m, dir: Ivan Villamel)

On a cold winter night, Laura reads her brother David the story of a strange creature that attacks children. Suddenly, a shiver runs Laura's body, feeling a strange presence in the house. It's him.

Sci-Fi Films Block 1

Brute Sanity (USA, 82m, dir: Sam Vanivray)

An FBI-trained neuropsychologist teams up with a thief to find a reality-altering device while her insane ex-boss unleashes bizarre traps to stop her.

The Online Date (USA, 7m, dir: Jimmy Matlosz)

A man experiences a really weird first date.

Tilting at Skyscrapers (USA, 8m, dir: Frank Stasio)

When a gamer is overcome by his obsession, his neighbor must shepherd him home.

Sci-Fi Films Block 2

Cronus (USA, 91m, dir: Derek Presley)

A genius recluse with amnesia awakens to find he has built a machine that extracts memories from the dead. He uses those memories to discover who he is and to rebuild a perfect past for himself.

Reactionary (USA, 11m, dir: Gary Taylor)

Two lab scientists discover an object hurtling towards the planet. They must determine what it is and how to stop it.

Sci-Fi Films Block 3

Illegal Aliens (USA, 10m, dir: Justin & Kristin Schaack)

A sci-fi comedy satire that's ironically human! Due to the recent arrival of undocumented immigrants, the city of Simpletown holds a special session city council meeting to determine if the town should officially ban the newcomers.

Show No Mercy (USA, 10m, dir: Scott Conditt)

A retro-arcade sci-fi action short film featuring Martin Kove (the bad guy from *The Karate Kid!*) and Jesse Kove (*The Last Race*)! Are you ready, players? *Show No Mercy!*

The Secret of Tatooine (France, 12m, dir: Jordan Inconstant)

Obi-wan Kenobi is exiled on Tatooine to watch over the young Luke Skywalker. His mission will be complicated when the young boy leaves alone in the desert in pursuit of the Tuskens. In saving him, Obi-wan stirred the curiosity of a bounty hunter and troops of the empire. Will the Knight Jedi succeed in preserving his identity while protecting Luke? This short film takes place between Episodes 3 and 4.

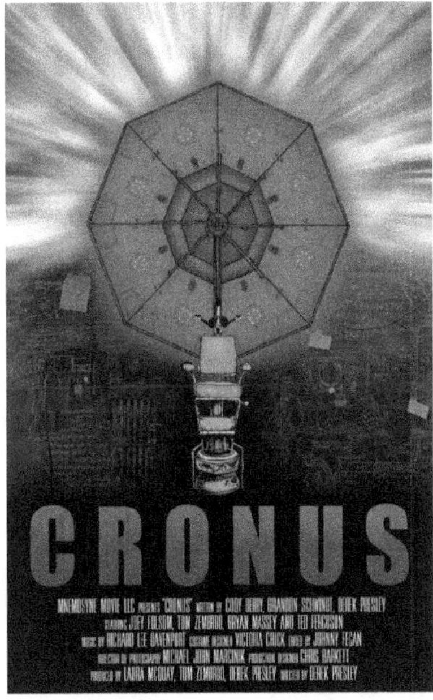

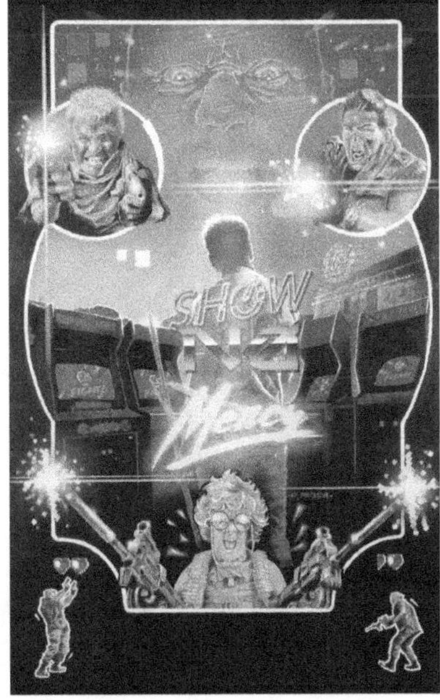

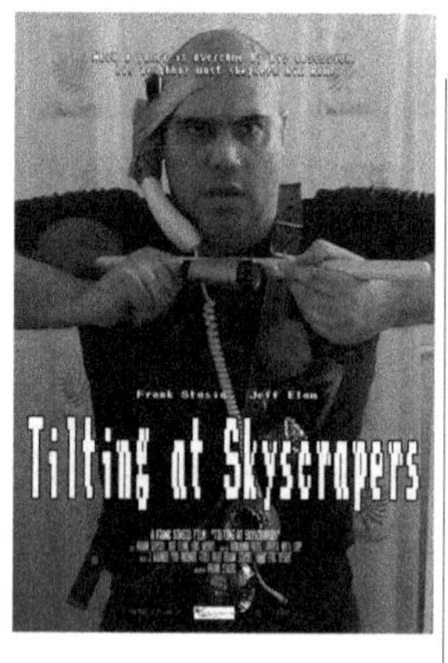

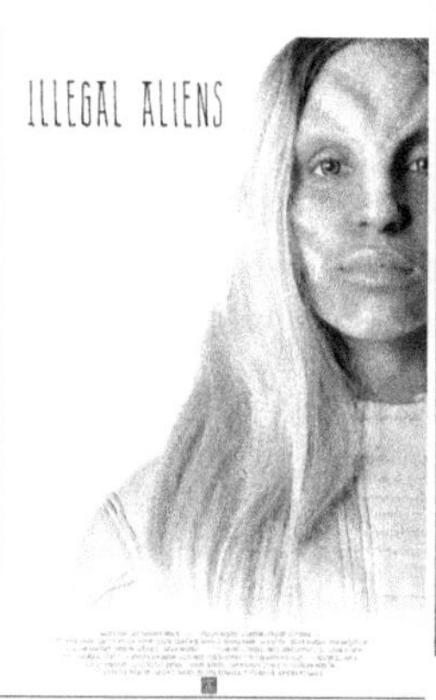

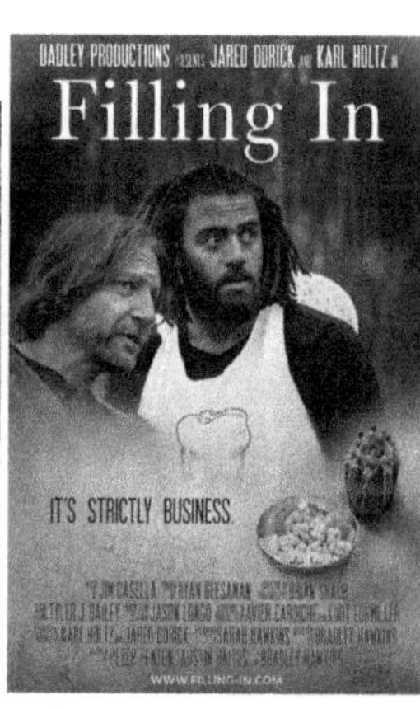

A Room (Hong Kong, 22m, dir: Chong Ming)

A man has changed to another job in order to make more money to marry his fiancée. One day he discovers the secret of a certain room in his company. This secret, which only appears after he gets off work, changes their relationship forever.

Filling In (USA, 22m, dir: Bradley Hawkins)

A gentle giant of a man, down on his luck, considers a risky and covert career path. To help him learn the ropes, a grizzled vet in the field takes him under his wing.

—Jon Bonnell
Film Festival Director

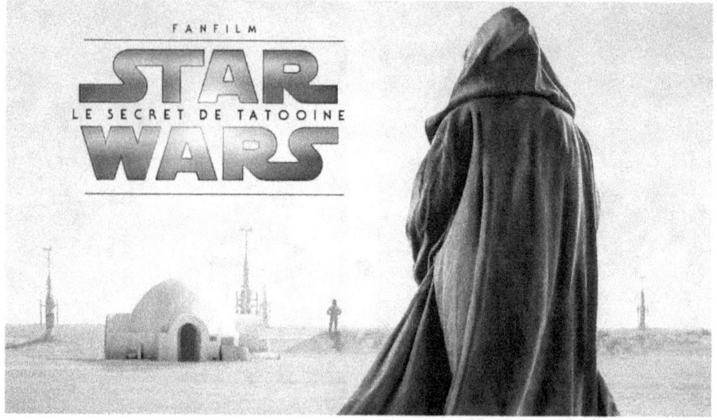

Gaming Hall

Get your game on! It's game time at Westercon's CONflagration Gaming Event for 2017! We will have everything you're looking for: role-playing, board games, minis, card games and much more; including a LARP, a Miniature Painting workshop, the Artemis Bridge Simulator and demos of virtual reality experiences via Oculus Rift!

If you are a new player, our events are run by trained volunteers who are enthusiastic to share their love of the hobby with you and your friends. You will also have a chance to play and interact with our special guests, the creators of your favorite games, like Ken St. Andre, creator of *Tunnels and Trolls*. We are proud to feature the vendors Isle of Games and Laughing Moon Productions right in the room!

Westercon's Gaming Room is located in the Abbey North and South on the west side of the hotel near the parking lot (and Rúla Búla restaurant). The games featured in the room will be PG-13+ (and up) so under 13s need to be accompanied by a parent or guardian. We are providing kid-friendly events for parents with kids to provide family entertainment for all ages.

Artemis Spaceship Bridge Simulator

Artemis Spaceship Bridge Simulator lets you and your friends assume the jobs of Captain, Helm, Science, Communication, Engineering and Weapon Control. Together you operate your ship and defend the sector from evil aliens. Artemis will be starting a new game every hour on the hour, starting at 9am everyday. We will have signup sheets in the room.

Oculus Rift VR Experience

Step into the next generation of gaming! Oculus radically redefines digital entertainment. We will be conducting short demonstrations of an Oculus Rift virtual reality headset. The exact applications are yet to be determined, but they will range from 360 degree environments and movies to interactive experiences and games. We will have signup sheets in the gaming room.

Saturday Morning Cartoon Games Event

We'll kick off the convention with a pair of roleplaying games that relate to cartoons. Join us for *Dungeons and Dragons: The Animated Series* and *Go Action Fun Time*! Plus we'll have some boardgames, featuring TMNT and *Scooby-Doo Mysteries: Haunted House Mystery* and *Scooby-Doo! Fright at the Fun Park*. Adults, teens, and kids with parents are welcome to come play.

Branum Games will be presenting a couple of gaming panels this year. As a successfully growing indie game company, they are sharing what they have learned about the gaming industry, Kickstarters and being an indie company. Read about the panels and sign up in the Gaming Hall.

Hours

We will open each morning at 9.00am, and close each day from 1.00pm to 2.00pm for a lunch break and 6.00pm to 7.00pm for a dinner break. The game room is currently scheduled to close for the night at 11.00pm, but if there is sufficient interest we will stay open into the wee hours.

If so, welcome to "Dawn of the Dice" Gaming Lounge, Late Night Gaming with Earl! He'll be running Catalyst Game Lab games (*Valiant Universe* and *Rockets & Rayguns, Cosmic Patrol*) after midnight on Saturday night, Chaosium Inc. games (*Call of Cthulhu: A Time of Harvest* Organized Play Campaign) after midnight on Sunday night, and Frog God games (*Grimmsgate* Introductory Module for *Swords & Wizardry*) after midnight on Monday night.

— Capt. Earl C. Hedges
Gaming Room Director

Gaming Schedule

Saturday (Daytime) - Abbey South

Start	End	Game	Run By
9.00am	11.00am	*TMNT: Shadows of the Past*	Isle of Games - Schretz
9.00am	11.00am	*Scooby-Doo! Mystery Mansion*	Holy Ghost
9.00am	11.00am	*Dixit*	Jason Youngdale
9.00am	1.00pm	*Go Action Fun Time*	Tony Padegimas
9.00am	1.00pm	*Dungeons & Dragons: The Animated Series*	Captain Hedges
9.00am	1.00pm	*Dead Rock Stars vs. The Cult of Bieber*	Jim Miller
9.00am	1.00pm	Demo for Steve Jackson Games	Oshiah, Ro, Gloryhoundd
9.00am	1.00pm	*Laughing Moon: Wheelhouse*	Todd VanHooser
11.00am	1.00pm	*Scooby-Doo! Fright and the Fun Park*	Holy Ghost
11.00am	1.00pm	*House Monsters*	Tiffany Branum, Jonathan Jackson
11.00am	1.00pm	*Nocturnes*	Tiffany Branum, Jonathan Jackson
1.00pm	2.00pm	Lunch Break	
2.00pm	4.00pm	*Rex: Final Days of an Empire*	Noah Richman
2.00pm	6.00pm	*Troll Hunters Wanted!*	Oshiah, Ro, Gloryhoundd
2.00pm	6.00pm	*House Monsters*	Tiffany Branum, Jonathan Jackson
2.00pm	6.00pm	*Nocturnes*	Tiffany Branum, Jonathan Jackson
2.00pm	6.00pm	*Star Trek Catan*	Holy Ghost
2.00pm	6.00pm	*Classic BattleTech* Mini Game Demos	Isle of Games - Schretz
2.00pm	6.00pm	*Fortune and Glory*	Isle of Games - Captain Vimes Drew
2.00pm	6.00pm	*Tunnels and Trolls*	Ken St. Andre, James St. Andre
4.00pm	6.00pm	*51st State*	Isle of Games - Captain Vimes Drew
6.00pm	7.00pm	Dinner Break	
7.00pm	9.00pm	*Action Movie World*	Jim Miller
7.00pm	9.00pm	*House Monsters*	Tiffany Branum, Jonathan Jackson
7.00pm	9.00pm	*Nocturnes*	Tiffany Branum, Jonathan Jackson
7.00pm	11.00pm	*Shadowrun Missions First Taste* Demo	Captain Hedges
7.00pm	11.00pm	*Conan*	Noah Richman
7.00pm	11.00pm	*Darkness Abides*	Bruce W. Soul
7.00pm	11.00pm	*WarMachine* and *Hordes* Demos	Isle of Games - Schretz
7.00pm	11.00pm	Demo for Steve Jackson Games	Oshiah, Ro, Gloryhoundd
11.00pm		Abbey South closes	

Saturday (Evening), Sunday (Morning) - Abbey North

Start	End	Game	Run By
7.00pm	11.00pm	*Houses of the Blooded* LARP	Chelsea Kelsey, Michael Falinski
12.00am	2.00am	*Shadow Hunters*	Noah Richman
12.00am	6.00am	*Valiant Universe* RPG	Captain Hedges
12.00am	6.00am	*Rockets and Rayguns, Cosmic Patrol*	Captain Hedges
2.00am	4.00am	*Spyfall*	Noah Richman

Sunday (Daytime) - Abbey South

Start	End	Game	Run By
9.00am	11.00am	*Saloon Tycoon*	Isle of Games - Captain Vimes Drew
9.00am	1.00pm	*Game of Thrones: Westeros Intrigue*	Jason Youngdale
9.00am	1.00pm	*House Monsters*	Tiffany Branum, Jonathan Jackson
9.00am	1.00pm	*Nocturnes*	Tiffany Branum, Jonathan Jackson
11.00am	1.00pm	*Action Movie World*	Jim Miller
11.00am	1.00pm	*Grimslingers*	Isle of Games - Captain Vimes Drew
11.00am	1.00pm	*Laughing Moon: Wheelhouse*	Todd VanHooser
1.00pm	2.00pm	Lunch Break	
2.00pm	4.00pm	*Doomtown: Reloaded*	Isle of Games - Captain Vimes Drew
2.00pm	4.00pm	*Laughing Moon: Wheelhouse*	Todd VanHooser
2.00pm	4.00pm	*Illuminati*	Travis Works
2.00pm	6.00pm	*House Monsters*	Tiffany Branum, Jonathan Jackson
2.00pm	6.00pm	*Nocturnes*	Tiffany Branum, Jonathan Jackson
2.00pm	6.00pm	*Wiz-War*	Noah Richman
2.00pm	6.00pm	*Tunnels and Trolls*	Ken St. Andre, James St. Andre
2.00pm	6.00pm	Demo for Steve Jackson Games	Oshiah, Ro, Gloryhoundd
4.00pm	6.00pm	*Illuminati*	Travis Works
6.00pm	7.00pm	Dinner Break	
7.00pm	11.00pm	*Fiasco on Flight 1180*	Travis Works
7.00pm	11.00pm	*House Monsters*	Tiffany Branum, Jonathan Jackson
7.00pm	11.00pm	*Nocturnes*	Tiffany Branum, Jonathan Jackson
7.00pm	11.00pm	*Laughing Moon: Wheelhouse*	Todd VanHooser
7.00pm	11.00pm	*Eclipse Space Battle*	Isle of Games - Captain Vimes Drew
7.00pm	11.00pm	*Cry Havoc*	Noah Richman
7.00pm	11.00pm	*Go Action Fun Time*	Tony Padegimas
7.00pm	11.00pm	*Darkness Abides*	Bruce W. Soul
11.00pm		Abbey South closes	

Painting Game Figurines

Sessions in Abbey North from 2.00pm to 4.00pm on Saturday, Sunday and Monday

Learn how to paint miniatures in Abbey North, led by Michael Duckett, Sr. Painting techniques will be described, then participants get to try! Great workshop for anyone wanting to learn how to paint miniatures. Adults, teens, and kids with parents are welcome to come and paint.

Sunday (Evening), Monday (Morning) - Abbey North

Start	End	Game	Run By
7.00pm	11.00pm	*Houses of the Blooded* LARP	Chelsea Kelsey, Michael Falinski
12.00am	6.00am	*Call of Cthulhu: A Time of Harvest*	Captain Hedges
12.00am	6.00am	*Good Cop Bad Cop*	Noah Richman

Monday (Daytime) - Abbey South

Start	End	Game	Run By
9.00am	11.00am	*Dungeon!*	Jason Youngdale
9.00am	11.00am	*Scooby-Doo! Mystery Mansion*	Holy Ghost
9.00am	1.00pm	*Scooby-Doo! Cthulhu*	Captain Hedges
		Scooby-Doo vs. Cthulhu: Down in the Bayou	Captain Hedges
9.00am	1.00pm	*Pulp City*	Isle of Games - Captain Vimes Drew
11.00am	1.00pm	*Scooby-Doo! Fright at the Fun Park*	Holy Ghost
11.00am	1.00pm	*Laughing Moon: Wheelhouse*	Todd VanHooser
1.00pm	2.00pm	Lunch Break	
2.00pm	4.00pm	*Laughing Moon: Wheelhouse*	Todd VanHooser
2.00pm	6.00pm	*Tunnels and Trolls*	Ken St. Andre, James St. Andre
2.00pm	6.00pm	Demo for Steve Jackson Games	Oshiah, Ro, Gloryhoundd
2.00pm	6.00pm	*Merchants & Marauders*	Noah Richman
6.00pm	7.00pm	Dinner Break	
7.00pm	11.00pm	*Fiasco on Flight 1180*	Travis Works
7.00pm	11.00pm	*House Monsters*	Tiffany Branum, Jonathan Jackson
7.00pm	11.00pm	*Nocturnes*	Tiffany Branum, Jonathan Jackson
7.00pm	11.00pm	*Go Action Fun Time*	Tony Padegimas
7.00pm	11.00pm	*Laughing Moon: Wheelhouse*	Todd VanHooser
7.00pm	11.00pm	*Runequest Glorantha*	Captain Hedges
7.00pm	11.00pm	*Star Trek Catan*	Holy Ghost
11.00pm		Abbey South closes	

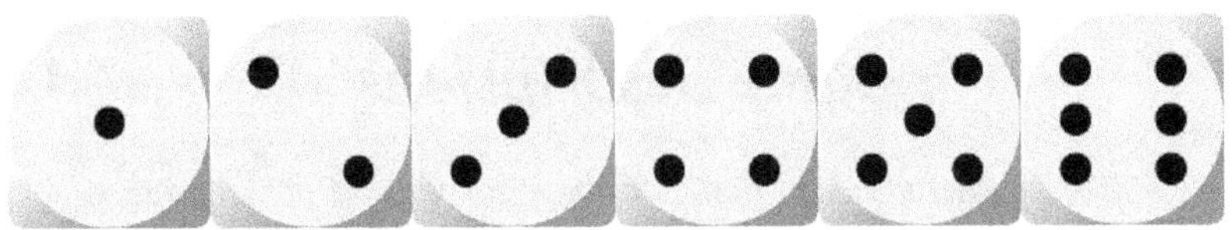

Monday (Evening), Tuesday (Morning) - Abbey North

Start	End	Game	Run By
12.00am	6.00am	*Swords & Wizardry: Grimmsgate*	Captain Hedges

Tuesday (Daytime) - Abbey South

Start	End	Game	Run By
9.00am	11.00am	*Xtronaut*	Holy Ghost
9.00am	11.00am	*Total War*	Travis Works
9.00am	1.00pm	*Colt Express*	Holy Ghost
9.00am	1.00pm	*Sherlock Holmes Consulting Detective: The Thames Murders & Other Cases*	Captain Hedges
9.00am	1.00pm	*Go Action Fun Time*	Tony Padegimas
9.00am	1.00pm	*House Monsters*	Tiffany Branum, Jonathan Jackson
9.00am	1.00pm	*Nocturnes*	Tiffany Branum, Jonathan Jackson
11.00am	1.00pm	*Total War*	Travis Works
11.00am	1.00pm	*Tiny Epic Kingdoms*	Noah Richman

Game Descriptions

Here are details of the games we have scheduled this weekend.

51st State

Saturday 4.00pm-6.00pm - Abbey South

Players take control of one of four factions vying for control of the post-war remains of a devastated United States. These factions struggle to build their stockpiles of supplies through conquest, trade, and expansion of their territory, until they achieve the stability needed to become the 51st State - and provide the foundation of a new society. For 2-4 players.

Action Movie World

Saturday 7.00pm-9.00pm, Sunday 11.00am-1.00pm - Abbey South

Action Movie World is powered by the Apocalypse RPG engine. It's a 1980s action movie; bring your cheesy one liners. The system is easy to learn and you just need to know the tropes of 80s action movies and a love of bad montage scenes.

Call of Cthulhu: A Time of Harvest

Monday 12.00am-6.00pm - Abbey North

You play a Miskatonic University student in 1929, undertaking research into folklore and a geological study under the direction of Professor Roger Harrold of the Anthropology Department. Your job is to assist him in a research project cataloging the folklore of Massachusetts, New Hampshire and Vermont...

Classic BattleTech Mini Game Demos

Saturday 2.00pm-6.00pm - Abbey South

The *BattleTech* game system takes you into the world of the 31st Century, where war has become a way of life. You are a MechWarrior, in command of the most powerful machine on the battlefield, and hold the fate of empires in your hand!

Colt Express

Tuesday 9.00am-1.00pm - Abbey South

On the 11th of July, 1899 at 10 a.m., the Union Pacific Express has left Folsom, New Mexico, with 47 passengers on board. After a few minutes, gunfire and hurrying footsteps on the roof can be heard. Heavily armed bandits have come to rob honest citizens of their wallets and jewels. Will they succeed in stealing the suitcase holding the Nice Valley Coal Company's weekly pay, despite it having been placed under the supervision of Marshal Samuel Ford? Will these bandits hinder one another more than the Marshal since only the richest one of them can come out on top? In *Colt Express*, you play a bandit robbing a train at the same time as other bandits and your goal is to become the richest outlaw of the Old West. At the end of the game, whoever fired the most bullets receives a $1,000 braggart bonus, and whoever bagged the richest haul wins!

Conan

Saturday 7.00pm-11.00pm - Abbey South

Based in the *Conan* universe, this is a scenario-based semi-cooperative asymmetric miniatures board game. One player is the Opponent, and the other players are Conan and his companions. The game is based purely on Robert E. Howard's novels and short stories. For 2-5 players.

Cry Havoc

Sunday 7.00pm-11.00pm - Abbey South

Cry Havoc is a card-driven, asymmetric, area control board game set in a new sci-fi universe. Deep in a quadrant of space believed to be empty, an unexplored planet has been discovered by three unique, powerful species. The resources of the planet are abundant beyond belief, but are protected vigorously by the indigenous species, known as the Trogs. Each player commands one of four unique factions, with varying abilities and units, that fight to gather the most resources. For 2-4 players.

Darkness Abides

Saturday 7.00pm-11.00pm, Sunday 7.00pm-11.00pm - Abbey South

A *Dungeons & Dragons* 5th Edition game, rated PG-13+. For 2-5 players.

Dead Rock Stars vs. The Cult of Bieber

Saturday 9.00am-1.00pm - Abbey South

This is a *Fate Accelerated* game in which David Bowie, Lemmy Kilmister, Prince, Rick James and Elvis return to save the world from the Cult of Bieber. Max of 3-5 Players. Ages 13+.

Demo for Steve Jackson Games

Saturday 9.00am-1.00pm, 7.00pm-11.00pm - Abbey South

Sunday 2.00pm-6.00pm, Monday 2.00pm-6.00pm - Abbey South

Dixit

Saturday 9.00am-11.00am - Abbey South

One player selects a card from their hand and speaks a word, phrase or sentence represented by the picture. The others then play a card which best represents what was said. The cards are revealed and each player votes for the best image. *Dixit* is suitable for adults and children, anyone who shares a love for stories. For 3-6 players.

Doomtown: Reloaded

Sunday 2.00pm-4.00pm - Abbey South

It's your chance to take it to the streets of Gomorra and show who runs the most dangerous boomtown in the West, the Weird West! *Doomtown* is an expandable card game set in the *Deadlands* universe and is a fast-paced game of gun slingin', spell slingin' and mud-slingin'! Use poker hands and card pulls for everything from gunfights to summoning abominations. Who will control the town? For 1-6 players.

Dungeon!

Monday 9.00am-11.00am - Abbey South

In many ways *Dungeon!* is similar to *Dungeons & Dragons*, although much simplified and transformed into a board game. Players explore a dungeon that is divided into levels of increasing difficulty, fighting monsters for valuable treasure. As players venture deeper into the dungeon, monsters become more difficult and the treasure more valuable. Several character classes each have slightly different fighting abilities - most notably the wizard, who can cast spells. Combat is simulated using dice; players roll the dice to attack a monster and, if unsuccessful, the dice are rolled to determine the effect of the monster's counter-attack. For 1-8 players.

Dungeons and Dragons: The Animated Series

Saturday 9.00am-1.00pm - Abbey South

It's time for a Saturday Morning Cartoon show using the ever-popular D&D 3.5 rules. Play as the kids Hank the Ranger, Diana the Acrobat, Eric the Cavalier, Presto the Magician, Sheila the Thief, Bobby the Barbarian and Uni the Unicorn as they fight against the evil forces of Venger, trying to find a way home. This special roleplay episode, *Beneath the Blade of the Sword Mountain*, is a short D&D adventure designed as a prelude to the opening of *A Dragon's Graveyard*. This event is set up for 4-7 players and adults, teens, and kids with parents are welcome to come play.

Eclipse Space Battle

Sunday 7.00pm-11.00pm - Abbey South

You're in control of a vast interstellar civilization, competing for success with its rivals. You will explore new star systems, research technologies, and build spaceships with which to wage war. There are many potential paths to victory, so plan your strategy according to the strengths and weaknesses of your species, while paying attention to the other civilizations' endeavors. The shadows of the great civilizations are about to eclipse the galaxy. Lead your people to victory! For 2-6 players.

Fiasco on Flight 1180

Sunday 7.00pm-11.00pm, Monday 7.00pm-11.00pm - Abbey South

A free-form game inspired by cinematic tales of small time capers gone disastrously wrong. It may start 15,000 feet in the sky, but will probably land in a disaster of the players' own making. Ages 13+. Max 5 players.

Fortune and Glory

Saturday 2.00pm-6.00pm - Abbey South

It is the late 1930s and the world is in turmoil. Humanity is on the brink of war as imperialist nations in the Far East and Europe work aggressively to expand their domination. The Nazis have taken control of Germany and now spread darkness across the globe in their hunt for powerful occult artifacts that can give them the upper hand in the days to come. Heroic adventurers from around the world answer the call racing against time to hunt down ancient artifacts, explore deadly temples and fight back the powers of darkness from engulfing the world in flames. It is a race of good versus evil and only a cunning and agile explorer can claim the ultimate prize of... *Fortune and Glory*. For 2-6 players.

Game of Thrones: Westeros Intrigue

Sunday 9.00am-1.00pm - Abbey South

Experience all the deadly intrigue of the King's Landing court in this fast-paced card game based on HBO's *Game of Thrones* series. Players must use their cunning and guile to claim the Iron Throne by enlisting the aid of notable members of the King's Landing court. If you plan ahead and play carefully, you may sit on the Iron Throne. For 2-6 players.

Go Action Fun Time

Saturday 9.00am-1.00pm, Sunday 7.00pm-11.00pm - Abbey South

Monday 7.00pm-11.00pm, Tuesday 9.00am-1.00pm - Abbey South

Go Action Fun Time is a role-playing game recreating Saturday morning (or now, late-night) action/adventure science-fantasy cartoon shows - only the kind you would actually want to watch. For 3-8 players.

Good Cop Bad Cop

Monday 12.00am-6.00pm - Abbey North

Good Cop Bad Cop is a 52 card hidden identity, deduction game where each player plays a law enforcement officer in a corrupt district. Players must investigate others to figure out who is on their side, grab one of the 2-3 guns on the table and shoot the opposing leader to win the game.

Grimslingers

Sunday 11.00am-1.00pm - Abbey South

In a land beyond God's reckonin' is a place called the Forgotten West - a cursed land in the American frontier. The Iron Witch has turned you into Grimslingers, powerful witches imbued with metal, machine, and fancy elemental powers - and now you must duel each other. For 2-6 players.

House Monsters

Saturday 11.00am-1.00pm, 2.00pm-6.00pm, 7.00pm-9.00pm - Abbey South

Sunday 9.00am-1.00pm, 2.00pm-6.00pm, 7.00pm-11.00pm - Abbey South

Monday 7.00pm-11.00pm, Tuesday 9.00am-1.00pm - Abbey South

This is a cute, fast card game for players of all ages. Easy to learn, try it out! For 6-10 players.

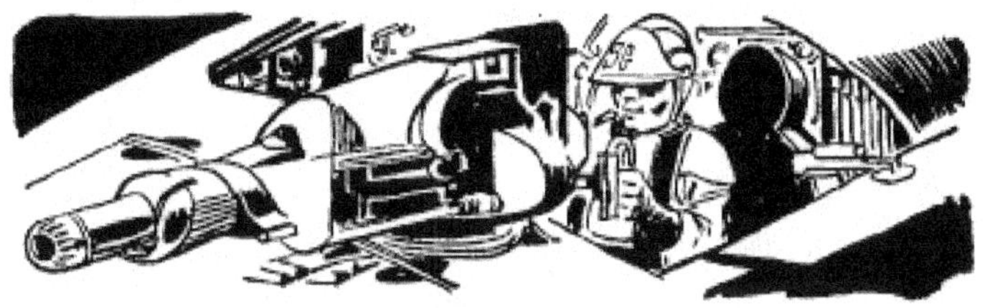

Houses of the Blooded LARP Outlands

Saturday 7.00pm-11.00pm - Abbey North

Sunday 7.00pm-11.00pm - Abbey North

Play one of the noble Ven as they play their games of power over the course of a seasonal celebration. The host is a newcomer to noble society and their lands are rich with treasure. Will you ally yourself with them to get access to the riches or will you ally with others to plunder them for yourself? Adults and teens 13+ are welcome to play.

Illuminati

Sunday 2.00pm-4.00pm, 4.00pm-6.00pm - Abbey South

Compete to take control of groups ranging from the FBI and CIA to the Dentists, increasing their wealth and power for further takeovers. Every player has different victory conditions and no stratagem is too devious as you scheme your way to victory! Ages 13+. Max 5 players.

Laughing Moon: Wheelhouse

Saturday 9.00am-1.00pm - Abbey South

Sunday 11.00am-1.00pm, 2.00pm-4.00pm, 7.00pm-11.00pm - Abbey South

Monday 11.00am-1.00pm, 2.00pm-4.00pm, 7.00pm-11.00pm - Abbey South

Wheelhouse is a post-apocalyptic fantasy RPG set thousands of years after a cataclysmic event shattered the world of Mythren and left the magical races virtually extinct. Players awaken a character imbued with the consciousness of a long-dead hero. As a group, the characters are sent beyond the civilized Twelve Towns and into the devastated "out-world" to serve a singular purpose given to them by the mysterious structure known simply as the Wheelhouse.

Characters are pre-generated and experienced, but no player knowledge of the game or system is required.

Players should be 16+ and up. Game is for 2-4 players.

Merchants & Marauders

Monday 2.00pm-6.00pm - Abbey South

Live the life of an influential merchant or a dreaded pirate in the Caribbean during the Golden Age of Piracy. Seek your fortune through trade, rumor hunting, missions and, of course, plundering. Modify your ship, buy impressive vessels, load deadly special ammunition and hire specialist crew members. Will your captain gain eternal glory and immense wealth - or find his wet grave under the stormy surface of the Caribbean Sea? For 2-4 players.

Nocturnes

Saturday 11.00am-1.00pm, 2.00pm-6.00pm, 7.00pm-9.00pm - Abbey South

Sunday 9.00am-1.00pm, 2.00pm-4.00pm, 7.00pm-11.00pm - Abbey South

Monday 7.00pm-11.00pm, Tuesday 9.00am-1.00pm - Abbey South

This is an eerie tile-based tabletop game about keeping your sanity while exploring a shared nightmare with other players. For 2-6 players.

Pulp City

Monday 9.00am-1.00pm - Abbey South

Welcome to the *Pulp City* world where powerful heroes clash with evil villains! *Pulp City* is the precious child of our twisted minds. It is born of our love for both miniature games and comic books. It's fast, it's furious and smart. It's *The Good, the Bad and the Ugly* meets *Godzilla*. First, we invite you to play a game that is heroic and character driven. *Pulp City* does not create a new world; it recreates a storyline with familiar elements of our pulp, TV series, B-movies and comic books! For ages 13+. 2-4 players.

Rex: Final Days of an Empire

Saturday 2.00pm-4.00pm - Abbey South

The classic *Dune* board game given a new theme and streamlined rules to keep playtime in check. Set in Fantasy Flight Games' *Twilight Imperium* universe, *Rex* is an asymmetric game where players control different alien races, with distinct racial abilities, who must negotiate and fight with one another for control of Capitol City, the capital of a dying galactic empire over which your civilization aims to rule. For 3-6 players.

Rockets and Rayguns: Cosmic Patrol

Sunday 12.00am-6.00am - Abbey North

Cosmic Patrol is a roleplaying game set in a retro future based on the Golden Age of science fiction. If you've ever seen a cover from a classic sci-fi pulp, you have the idea. You and your friends form the crew of a Cosmic Patrol rocketship and blast off for action and adventure in the wild galaxy. Players take the role of Patrolmen, the first and last line of defense in a dangerous galaxy. Patrolmen explore, discover and defend the interests of humans wherever they go, with atomic ray guns at their hip.

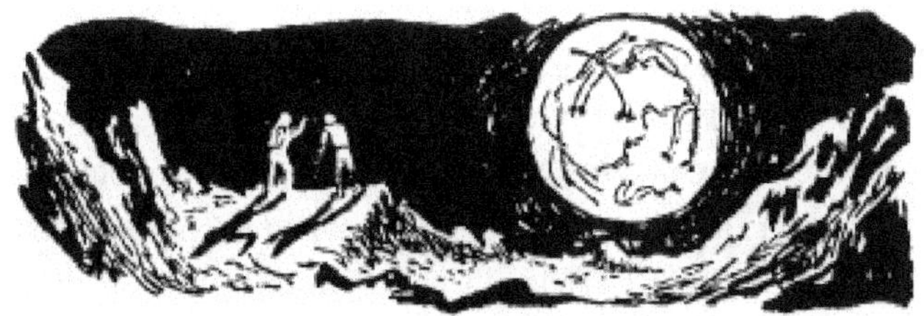

Runequest Glorantha

Monday 7.00pm-11.00pm - Abbey South

Come explore Glorantha, a Bronze Age world where mythology comes to life and adventure is only a step away. Glorantha is similar to our own world, but it exists in a magical universe where the laws of physics are subordinate to the whims of gods and spirits. To understand Glorantha, you must leave our mundane world and enter the world of myth. The Sun is a living god and not a nearby star. Countless gods exist, some even more powerful than the Sun, and all have the power to directly affect humanity. Rulers and leaders use magical not technological means to achieve their ends, and even the humblest will cross the paths of the gods and spirits.

Saloon Tycoon

Sunday 9.00am-11.00am - Abbey South

You own a simple saloon in an old west gold rush town but need to expand into a thriving center for commerce and entertainment. You'll need to attract wealthy and famous citizens of the town while keeping away the less savory characters. For 2-4 players.

Scooby Doo Cthulhu

Monday 9.00am-1.00pm - Abbey South

The Scooby Doo gang for *Call of Cthulhu: Mystery Mansion* roleplaying game using your favorite Scooby Doo characters.

Scenario 1: While the kids are visiting Boston, they read in the local newspaper that Andrew Keeling, a successful Boston businessman, has disappeared, and his family is offering a reward for information on his whereabouts! Can Mystery Inc. find him before it's too late? For 2-5 players. Kid friendly event with parent or guardian.

Scooby Doo vs. Cthulhu - Down in the Bayou

Monday 9.00am-1.00pm - Abbey South

Scenario 2: Louisiana, 1970. The Scooby gang get called out to a small town to investigate a little girl's disappearance. What will they find under the mask? For 2-5 players. Kid friendly event with parent or guardian.

Scooby-Doo! Fright at the Fun Park

Saturday 11.00am-1.00pm, Monday 11.00am-1.00pm - Abbey South

Jinkies! Can you help the Mystery Inc. gang save the fun park from a spooky ghoul? For ages 4+, kid-friendly event with parent or guardian. For 2-8 players.

Scooby-Doo! Mystery Mansion

Saturday 9.00am-11.00am, Monday 9.00am-11.00am - Abbey South

There's a monster lurking in the mystery mansion. If you're the first player to discover who it is and what they're doing to try to scare Scooby Doo and his friends, you win. Kid-friendly event with parent or guardian. For 2-4 players.

Shadowrun Missions: The First Taste Demo

Abbey South, Saturday 7.00pm-11.00pm

The First Taste is an introductory event for players who have never played *Shadowrun* or for those who haven't played in quite some time, e.g. since a previous edition. *The First Taste* is kept short (two hours); this way, individuals can just drop in and play without committing a large amount of time.

Shadow Hunters

Abbey North, Sunday 12.00am-2.00am

Shadow Hunters is a survival board game set in a devil-filled forest in which three groups of characters - the Shadows, creatures of the night; the Hunters, humans who try to destroy supernatural creatures; and the Neutrals, civilians caught in the middle of this ancient battle - struggle against each other to survive. You belong to one of these groups and must conceal your identity from others since you don't know whom you can trust - at least not initially. Over time, though, someone might decipher who you are through your actions or through Hermit cards, or you might even reveal yourself to use your special ability. The key to victory is to identify your allies and enemies early because once your identity is revealed, your enemies will attack with impunity using their special abilities like Demolish, Teleport and Suck Blood or their equipment cards such as the Rusty Broad Ax or Fortune Brooch. This ancient battle comes to a head and only one group will stand victorious - or a civilian, in the right circumstances, might claim victory.

The 2011 edition of *Shadow Hunters* from Z-Man Games includes the *Shadow Hunters Expansion*, a set of ten new characters previously sold separately.

Sherlock Holmes Consulting Detective: The Thames Murders & Other Cases

Abbey South, Tuesday 9.00am-1.00pm

Have you ever had the desire to walk the streets of Victorian London with Sherlock Holmes in search of Professor Moriarty? To search the docks for the giant rat of Sumatra? To walk up Baker Street as the fog is rolling in and hear Holmes cry out, "Come, Watson, come! The game is afoot!"? Now you can! You can enter the opium den beneath the Bar of Gold, but beware, that may be Colonel Sebastian Moran lurking around the corner. You can capture the mystery and excitement of Holmes's London in this challenging and informative game. You, the player, will match your deductive abilities against your opponents and the master sleuth himself, Sherlock Holmes.

In *Sherlock Holmes Consulting Detective*, you are presented with a mystery to solve, and it is then up to you to trace the threads of evidence through the byways and mansions of nineteenth century London. You will interview suspects, search the newspapers for clues, and put together the facts to reach a solution. Why were two lions murdered in Hyde Park? Who is responsible for the missing paintings from the National Gallery? Who murdered Oswald Mason and why? These are just a few of the cases that will challenge your ingenuity and deductive abilities.

This is not a board game: No dice, no luck, but a challenge to your mental ability. The game has been thoroughly researched for Holmesian and Victorian accuracy so as to capture a feeling of that bygone era.

Spyfall

Abbey North, Sunday 2.00am-4.00am

Spyfall is played over several rounds and, at the start of each round, all players receive cards showing the same location, except that one player receives a card that says 'Spy' instead of the location. Players then start asking each other questions, trying to guess who among them is the spy. The spy doesn't know where he is, so he has to listen carefully. When it's his time to answer, he'd better create a good story! After a few rounds of guessing, suspicion and bluffing, the game ends and whoever has scored the most points is victorious!

Star Trek Catan

Abbey South, Saturday 2.00pm-6.00pm, Monday 7.00pm-11.00pm

Space... the final frontier... *Star Trek Catan* combines the adventures of the legendary Starship Enterprise with those of the Settlers of Catan. The challenge is to settle a world that has never been settled before. 3 players wanted for this game, ages 13+.

Swords & Wizardry: Grimmsgate

Abbey North, Monday 12.00am-6.00am

Swords and Wizardry Light is a fast-play introduction to *Swords & Wizardry* and role-playing games in general. Ideal for introducing new players of any age to tabletop role-playing games. *Grimmsgate* is an introductory adventure for *Swords & Wizardry*.

Deep in the wooded wilderness, the village of Grimmsgate is an outpost town on a seldom-traveled trail, right at the edge of nowhere. The village's half-ruined temple of Law, dilapidated inn, drunken blacksmith, exiled trader and fur-trappers are enough to keep the bloody-minded denizens of the dark forest at bay, but nobody expects the village to still be there in another ten years. The woods have become too dangerous for the trappers who once caught animals for fur, and merchants no longer travel the poorly-maintained road. What great evil and what fabulous treasures are to be found in these lands? A brave band of adventurers might make their fortunes here. Or perhaps they might never return...

Tiny Epic Kingdoms

Abbey South, Saturday 9.00am-11.00am

Explore lands and factions, expand kingdoms, exploit opportunities and exterminate all those who question your rule... but so will everyone else! The results of this tiny conflict are nothing short of epic! Surprisingly simple yet deeply engaging and, with 13 unique and thematic factions and 16 unique territories, no game will ever be the same. For 1-5 players.

TMNT: Shadows of the Past

Abbey South, Saturday 9.00am-11.00am

Battle with your brothers through the streets of NYC to defend your town from Shredder's Foot Clan. *TMNT: Shadows of the Past* is a scenario-driven adventure boardgame. Kid-friendly event. For 1-4 players.

Total War

Abbey South, Tuesday 9.00am-11.00am, 11.00am-1.00pm

Two simple card games - the classic game of *Naval War* and a new quick-to-play card game *Battlefront* - played at the same time. Because every good general needs to be able to multi-task! Ages 16+. For 2-5 players.

Troll Hunters Wanted!

Abbey South, Saturday 2.00pm-6.00pm

The town of Corpse Hollow has a troll infestation. They also have coin to pay mercenaries! You just happen to need some cash and have a knack for dealing with other people's problems. This is a continuing Dungeon Fantasy Adventure adventure for experienced *GURPS* players with an emphasis on hack and slash over role-playing. Bring your 200 point DF character or one will be provided. For 3-8 players.

Tunnels and Trolls

Abbey South, Saturday, Sunday and Monday 2.00pm-6.00pm

Come play with Ken St. Andre, the designer of one the best RPGs ever. Ages PG-13 and up, for 3-6 players. Ken's son James will be running an overflow table as needed, also 3-6 players.

Valiant Universe

Abbey North, Sunday 12.00am-6.00am

Do you have what it takes? No matter the powers, no matter the choices, the price in body and mind may be more than you're willing to pay. And your choices will lead to heroics... or to villainy. In the *Valiant Universe* RPG, players will immerse themselves in a dark and gritty world where every mission and every battle has deadly consequences. Whether playing X-O Manowar, Bloodshot, Shadowman or even the all-powerful Toyo Harada - or any of dozens of characters - Valiant's most fearless heroes will unite for the first time in a role-playing game, allowing you to join their stories and create new ones!

WarMachine and Hordes Demos

Abbey South, Saturday 7.00pm-11.00pm

Want to learn how to play the new *WarMachine* and *Hordes* Mk III rules? Schretz from Isle of Games will be running demos. Adults and teens 13+ are welcome to play.

Wiz-War

Abbey South, Sunday 2.00pm-6.00pm

Wizards wage no-spells-barred magical duels deep in an underground labyrinth. This classic board game of magical mayhem pits players' wizards against each other in a stupendous struggle for magical mastery. The last wizard standing always wins. For 2-4 players.

Xtronaut

Abbey South, Tuesday 9.00am-11.00am

Rocket science for everyone! Capturing the real-world thrill and challenges of planetary exploration, Xtronaut™: The Game of Solar System Exploration gives 2-4 players, ages 7 and up, the chance to develop space missions and explore the solar system. The game is based on real planetary missions and rocket science. It also contains elements of politics and strategy that are inspired by the real-life situations that space missions face.

Special Events

Friday

Start	End	Event	Location
6.00pm		Happy Hour Mixer	Rúla Búla Irish Pub and Restaurant
7.00pm	8.30pm	Apocalypse Later Mini-Film Festival #26	Xavier

Saturday

Start	End	Event	Location
12.00pm	1.00pm	DREAD Fleet: Freshwater Follies Comedy Show	Palm E/F
2.30pm	3.30pm	Tim Griffin Concert	Palm E/F
4.00pm	5.00pm	Opening Ceremonies	Palm E/F
5.00pm	7.00pm	Meet the Guests (Ice Cream Social)	ConSuite
7.00pm	9.00pm	Regency Dance	Palm E/F
7.00pm	11.00pm	Body Painting with Mark Greenawalt	Dolores
8.30pm	11.30pm	Evening Erotica with Gini Koch	Xavier

Sunday

Start	End	Event	Location
9.00am	1.00pm	Heinlein Society Blood Drive	Outside
12.30pm	2.30pm	At the Movies	Xavier
5.00pm	7.00pm	Artists' Reception	Palm B/C
8.00pm	10.00pm	Masquerade	Palm E/F

Monday

Start	End	Event	Location
1.30pm	3.30pm	Charity Auction	Cloister
4.00pm	5.00pm	Art Auction	Cloister
7.00pm	9.00pm	Three Toed Sock Hop	Palm E/F
8.00pm	11.00pm	Match Game	Xavier

Tuesday

Start	End	Event	Location
12.30pm	2.30pm	At the Movies: Indie Style	Wind Flower
5.00pm	6.00pm	Closing Ceremonies	Palm E/F
6.00pm		Dead Dog	ConSuite
9.00pm		Tempe 4th of July Fireworks Display	Pool Area

Friday (Preview Night)

Because so many attendees are flying in on Friday and will be staying at the hotel on Friday night, we've set up some preview night programming before the con begins to warm everyone up.

The Dealers' Room and Art Show will not be open on Friday, but the Filk room will. That's Joshua Tree and open filk is scheduled from 9.00pm.

Happy Hour Mixer

Friday 6.00pm-whenever, Rúla Búla Irish Pub and Restaurant

We'll be at Rúla Búla Irish Pub and Restaurant for a Happy Hour Mixer, starting around 6.00pm. This is right next door to the hotel; fall out of the Gaming Hall and you'll fall into Rúla Búla.

Fans of Kevin Hearne's *Iron Druid* book series will recognize Rúla Búla as a location; Atticus O'Sullivan ate fish n' chips here with Jesus.

Apocalypse Later Mini-Film Festival

Friday 7.00pm-8.30pm - Xavier - Hal C. F. Astell of Apocalypse Later

Hal C. F. Astell of Apocalypse Later programs and presents mini-film festivals at conventions across the southwest and this will be event #26. It's his fifth year running at LepreCon and his second Westercon (after two well-received sets at Westercon 68 in San Diego).

At Westercon 70, he'll present a curated 90 minute set of international award-winning science fiction and fantasy short films, some of which you can't see outside the film festival circuit.

The DREAD Fleet: Freshwater Follies Comedy Show

Saturday 12.00pm-1.00pm - Palm E/F - The DREAD Fleet

As our local pirate group, the DREAD Fleet, sail away to fresher waters, they encounter some witty and wily prohibition era river pirates! Laugh and learn about historical pirates of the great lakes and rivers of the US in the Freshwater Follies Comedy Show.

Tim Griffin Concert

Saturday 2.30pm-3.30pm - Palm E/F - Tim Griffin

Come and see our Filk Guest of Honor, Tim Griffin, performing live.

Opening Ceremonies

Saturday 4.00pm-5.00pm - Palm E/F - Weston Ochse, Guests of Honor

Westercon 70 officially opens at noon on Saturday, though some things will start earlier. However, our Opening Ceremonies are scheduled for 4.00pm to ensure that everyone who wants to be there can be.

Join our Toastmaster, Weston Ochse, as he introduces all our Guests of Honor and gets the ball officially rolling for Westercon 70.

Meet the Guests (Ice Cream Social)

Saturday 5.00pm-6.00pm - ConSuite - Guests of Honor

After the Opening Ceremonies, we'll shift upstairs to the ConSuite (room 2038) for our Meet the Guests event, where you can mingle and chat with the Guests of Honor that Weston Ochse just introduced.

While the Ice Cream Social is a Californian Westercon tradition, we feel that it's the best way to combat the 4th of July heat in Tempe too!

Regency Dance

Saturday 7.00pm-9.00pm - Palm E/F - Alex Canto, John Hertz

Every Westercon has two dances, one of them a Regency Dance. Ours is presented by John Hertz and our Dance Co-ordinator, Alex Canto.

Body Painting with Mark Greenawalt

Saturday 7.00pm-11.00pm - Dolores - Mark Greenawalt

Mark Greenawalt's live body painting demo will breathe life into a brand new original character. Model Griffin Maria will be transformed into the Hollow Queen from the new storyline from Todd VanHooser called *Wheelhouse*. **Restricted to 18+.**

Evening Erotica with Gini Koch

Saturday 8.30pm-11.30pm - Xavier - Gini Koch and friends

Join Gini Koch, her Official Mod with the Most (Sass) Edward Pulley, the Blushing Meter, Joseph Gaxiola, and Gini's special guests: author Tom Leveen and the Two Gay Geeks podcast, as they teach you how to play the Euphemism Game! Guaranteed to be your most rollicking event at Westercon (and that's saying a lot). You're also guaranteed a little learning and a LOT of great prizes! (So many prizes! SO MANY!) For those who've attended before, you know you never know what to expect, including who might show up to "assist" with the game. For those who've only heard about what this event is like, now's your chance to experience it first hand! So come join Gini and get your euphemisms on! **Restricted to 18+.**

Heinlein Society Blood Drive

Sunday, 9.00am-1.00pm - Sign up in the Lobby

Blood drives have been a tradition at sci-fi cons since Robert A. Heinlein started them at MidAmericon, the 34th World Science Fiction Convention, in 1976. Heinlein readers will recall the National Rare Blood Club was an integral part of his novel *I Will Fear No Evil* and, in an appendix to the novel, he informed his readers that the organization he had written about actually existed and deserved their support. Heinlein traveled extensively to promote this important cause and frequently donated himself.

The Heinlein Society has made blood drives a permanent, ongoing effort and continues to invite all to participate in this critically important effort. Life-saving blood is always in short supply, and a healthy person may donate every 56 days. According to the Red Cross, each blood donation can save up to three lives. It is a safe and quick procedure, usually taking no more than an hour of one's time.

While walk-ins are welcome, we'd appreciate as many as possible to pre-register. Our sign-up table will be in the Lobby. Thank you for paying it forward.

At the Movies

Sunday, 12.30pm-2.30pm - Xavier - Len Berger

This is a favorite convention panel at Arizona genre cons. You will get a sneak peak at trailers for some exciting upcoming movies then, after the trailers, we will hold a raffle for *free* movie promotional material (T-shirts, baseball caps, special posters and more). The late Barry Bard started this panel decades ago and we all miss Barry.

Sponsored by CASFS (Central Arizona Speculative Fiction Society).

Artists' Reception

Sunday, 5.00pm-7.00pm - Palm B/C - Displaying Artists

Come celebrate the artists who are displaying their work in our Art Show at an Artists' Reception, which will be hosted in our Art Show with courtesy snacks and a cash bar.

Masquerade

Sunday, 8.00pm-10.00pm - Palm E/F - Diana Given

No sci-fi con is complete without a Masquerade! Ours is being organized by Elaine Mami, of the Lower Arizona Costume Enthusiasts, and MC'd by Diana Given, who co-runs the Arizona Steampunk Society and Wild Wild West Steampunk Convention.

Setup will be 4.30pm-6.30pm in Palm E/F, with rehearsal from 6.30pm-7.30pm. Masquerade Green Room is Dolores, open 6.30pm onwards.

Charity Auction

Monday 1.30pm-2.30pm - Cloister - Jen McAlonan, J. B. Talbott

100% of the proceeds from our Charity Auction, organized by Catherine Book, will benefit the Challenger Space Center in Peoria, AZ.

Come and bid on a wide variety of books, hardcover and paperback, signed and unsigned, along with art proofs, jewelry, movie memorabilia, space posters and more. Program Guides will be available at Registration, listing all items under the hammer and details are also online.

Art Auction

Monday, 4.00pm-5.00pm - Cloister

Artwork displayed for auction that receives three or more written bids by the end of the Art Show will go to voice auction. The Art Auction is when this happens. Bid in the Art Show and bid higher at the Auction!

Three Toed Sock Hop

Monday 7.00pm-9.00pm - Palm E/F - Alex Canto

Our second dance is a Three Toed Sock Hop, on the theme that "Elvis is not dead; he just went home!" Put on your dancing shoes and get down with some tunes that are out of this world! No matter if your flying saucer's blown its top, cut a rug with the cool cats! Costumes encouraged but not required, from rockabilly Batman to elvish impersonators; just grab an extra safety pin so you don't lose your cool, and it stays securely attached. Beginner swing dance lesson at 7:30pm. There will be a cash bar.

Match Game

Monday 8.00pm-11.00pm - Xavier - Kevin Standlee

Get ready to match the fannish stars! In this re-creation of the classic 1970s game show, contestants are selected randomly from the audience to attempt to match the panelists' answers to fill-in-the-blank questions like "Captain Kirk has the biggest ___ in Starfleet!" Prizes for all contestants.

At the Movies - Indie Style

Tuesday 12.30pm-2.30pm - Wind Flower - Len Berger

This is a new flavor for an old favorite panel at Arizona genre cons. You will get a sneak peak at trailers for some exciting upcoming independent movies that may or may not end up in your local theater. After the trailers we will hold a raffle for *free* movie promotional material (T-shirts, baseball caps, special posters and more). Sponsored by CASFS.

Closing Ceremonies

Tuesday 5.00pm-6.00pm - Palm E/F - Weston Ochse, Guests of Honor

Even though we don't want the con to end, we have to wrap sometime. Join us as Toastmaster Weston Ochse ends Westercon 70 in style and our chair, Dee Astell, literally passes the Westercon gavel on to Nikki Ebright, who will chair Westercon 71 in Westminster, CO this time next year.

Dead Dog

Tuesday 6.00pm-whenever - ConSuite

You don't have to go home but you can't stay here! Well, actually you can. If you're not involved in taking down the event, then sit back and relax with new friends and old in the ConSuite.

Tempe 4th of July Fireworks

Tuesday 9.00pm-whenever, ConSuite, Pool Area (or anywhere)

Join us for TusCon 44!

November 10-12, 2017 in Tucson, Arizona

"The Best Little Sci-Fi, Fantasy, and Horror Convention in Arizona"

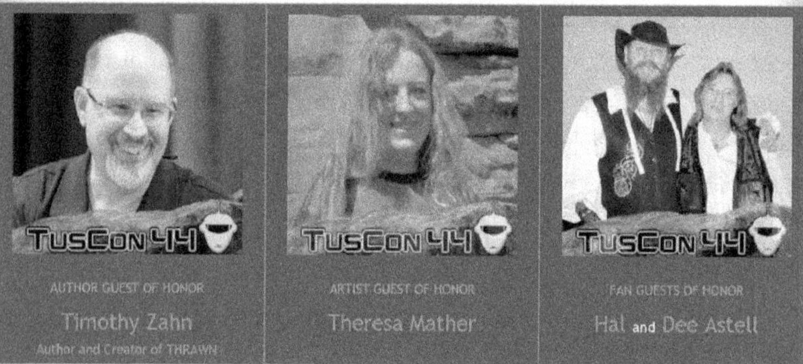

Featuring: Meet the Pros, Panels, Art Demos, Silent Auction, Dealers Room, Video Room, LAN and Tabletop Gaming, ConSuite, Masquerade, and more!

Buy your memberships early – last year's memberships sold out very early and are again limited to only 500!

Author Guest of Honor: Timothy Zahn, creator of THRAWN
Artist Guest of Honor: Theresa Mather
Fan Guests of Honor: Hal and Dee Astell
Toastmaster: Weston Ochse
Special Guest: Geoff Notkin
Special Guest Performers: Cirque des Bêtes
Masquerade Host: Madame Askew
Information: www.tusconscificon.com or basfa@earthlink.net

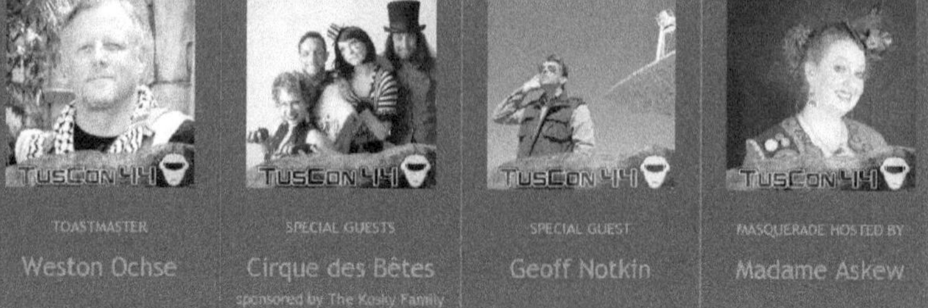

Panel Participants

Acoustically Sound

Acoustically Sound, also known as Gerry, Sandy, and Rhiannon Tyra, have been working sound support for music events since their first job at Westercon 52 (Spokane '99). Since then they have worked Worldcons, NorthAmericon, Westercons, FilkCons (from Atlanta to San Francisco Bay) and various conventions in between. Gerry and Sandy were Interfilk guests at FilKONtario in 2009.

Linda D. Addison

Linda D. Addison is the award-winning author of four collections, including *How to Recognize a Demon Has Become Your Friend*, and she is the first African-American recipient of the HWA Bram Stoker Award®. She has published over 300 poems, stories and articles and she is a member of CITH, HWA, SFWA and SFPA. Addison is one of the editors of *Sycorax's Daughters* (Cedar Grove Publishing), an anthology of horror by African-American women. Catch her latest work in anthologies *Scary Out There* (Simon & Schuster), *The Beauty of Death* (Independent Legions Publishing) and *Into Painfreak* (Necro Publications).

Allen Amis

Allen Amis is a costume and prop builder working out of Chandler, AZ. He got his start when *Star Wars* costuming ignited his passion for building and weathering sci-fi armor. He's won awards and accolades for his ability to bring artistic concepts and renderings to life as wearable costumes and displayable props. Most recently, his work has been featured with the video game powerhouse Bioware, *Nabucco* performed by Opera Theater of Montclair, Star Wars Celebration, and Ryan Tree's *Legacy* music video.

Anabel Amis

Anabel Amis in a concept artist from Chandler, AZ, whose work is inspired by an upbringing immersed in macabre fairy tales, video games and anime. She also moonlights as a project manager for the cosplay projects *Men vs. Cosplay* and *Women vs. Cosplay*, which feature professional and novice cosplayers from all around the world.

Capt. Ares

Capt. Ares has been participating in conventions since Del Webb's TowneHouse LepreCon in the 80s, and he's thrown many Corsair/pirate parties at LepreCon and CopperCon! He's been drumming since Estrella 3, and has taken lessons from the Master, Gabby Tawill. He specializes in middle-eastern music and teaches basic doumbek, djembe, zarb and doholla. Capt. Ares first became interested in drumming in the SCA for bellydancers and wanted to contribute. He's performed all over Arizona, and played in many groups, with many very talented musicians.

Madame Askew

Madame is a time traveling tea aficionado, obsessed with tea, fashion & the proper uses for headgear. While she is often the center of tea inspired escapades, especially tea duelling, and a great fan of compliment duelling, Madame loves nothing so much as meeting charming and talented individuals across time, throughout the universe and in tea houses wherever she may appear. When Madame is not preoccupied with tea, she operates a small atelier where she creates fanciful and charming bespoke garments for ladies and gentlemen.

Hal C. F. Astell

While he still has a day job, Hal C. F. Astell is a teacher by blood and a writer by the grace of the dread lord, which gradually transformed him into a film critic. He reviews movies at his own site, Apocalypse Later, which is celebrating its 10th anniversary in 2017, but has written for various others. He writes book reviews for the Nameless Zine.

The Apocalypse Later Empire grew from that site to encompass a publishing imprint (Apocalypse Later Press), the only dedicated annual genre film festival in the sixth largest city in the US (the Apocalypse Later International Fantastic Film Festival in Phoenix) and a string of mini-film festivals at conventions across the southwest.

Garrick & Jackie Backer

KnowOne's Designs consists of Garrick and Jackie Backer. They helped found the charity Project Hero, and through it volunteer for local comic shops. They love being a part of the community. Garrick does most of the dirty work i.e. working with power tools, molding and casting while Jackie mostly focuses on the sewing, make-up/fx and design aspect.

Kim Bailey

Over 40 years in the film industry, Kim Bailey had the honor to work with some of the most amazing individuals and to touch upon many different projects and genres. Those who know his contributions to the industry, know my work for projects like the 1988 TV series, *Star Trek: The Next Generation*'s "Borg Cube" and "Core Sample" (episode *Q-Who*), *Space Above and Beyond* for Fox, or for technology design on Brian DePalma's 1999 feature film, *Mission to Mars*.

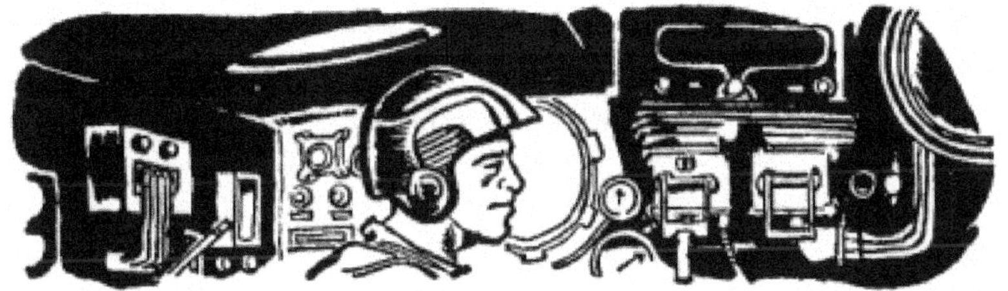

Jess Ballantyne

Jess Ballantyne is a a poet, an author, a bookworm and a mom. Her high school superlative was "Most Likely to Become a Math Teacher". Jess was most known in the poetry slam community for being a judge and, more recently, as a performer. Jess has performed in Phoenix, Mesa, Tempe and Sedona. She continues to visit open mikes and poetry slams across Arizona. Jess is an avid *Harry Potter* fan, Her house is Slytherin and her patronus is an Otter. She also is a *Game of Thrones* fan. She has read the books, and is glued to her HBO GO account every season. Jess is also an avid coffee drinker, loves fine cheeses and has a Zombie Apocalypse survival plan.

Colette Black

Colette Black writes New Adult and Young Adult sci-fi and fantasy novels with kick-butt characters, lots of action and always a touch of romance. Black is the author of the *Mankind's Redemption* series, including *Noble Ark* which won the 2014 Howey award for Best Complete Package. She's also the author of *Fourteen*, book one in *The Number Prophecy* series, and *Moon Shadows*, published by Brick Cave Media. Living in the far outskirts of Phoenix, AZ, she has myriad adventures with her family, two dogs, a mischievous cat, two hens, a cockatiel and the occasional unwanted scorpion.

Nathan Blackwell

Director, producer, writer, editor... (so basically) storyteller. As a filmmaker, Nathan Blackwell loves finding the comedy in every story and the humanity in every moment. He seeks what's outside the ordinary, hoping to discover fun and original ways to connect with people. With twenty years of filmmaking experience, he's directed two feature films, a dozen commercials, over forty short films and produced several web series.

Tia Bly

Tia is a local fan and graduate student at Arizona State University. Ask her about her favorite fantasy novels and K-dramas!

Jeff and Maya Bohnhoff

Jeff and Maya Bohnhoff have been playing music together for a long time. Their exact origins are lost in the mists of history, but most authorities seem to agree that they joined forces musically in 1979. For many years years, their true danger lay dormant, until in 1995 they encountered filk music, and it became clear what they were destined to do - ruin classic rock for as many people as they possibly could. To that end, Jeff, with occasional help from Maya, began an unabated spree of parodic crimes against the Beatles, the Who, Queen, Steely Dan and many others too numerous to count.

Their various crimes and offenses are documented in three albums of (mostly) classic rock parody - *Retro Rocket Science, Aliens Ate My Homework!* and *Grated Hits*. In order to elude pursuit, they also sometimes perform and record original songs, such as those on their albums *Manhattan Sleeps, Möbius Street* and *I Remember the Rain*. They have been known to brazenly perform both their parodies and original songs with nothing between them and potentially outraged audiences but acoustic guitars. Despite this, they have so far evaded serious injury.

Maya Bohnhoff

Writer of speculative fiction as the result of a horrible childhood incident involving Klaatu and a robot named Gort, Maya is the New York Times bestselling author of science fiction and fantasy including *Star Wars: The Last Jedi* (with Michael Reaves). Singer, songwriter, performer, Bahá'í. Her short fiction appearances include *Analog, Amazing Stories, Interzone,* and *Baen's Universe*; she's a Nebula, Crawford, Campbell, Sidewise and British Science Fiction award finalist.

Johnna Buttrick

Johnna Buttrick is an artist, crafter, cosplayer, costume designer and seamstress extraordinaire who has been causing chaos on the con scene for quite a few years now.

Ashley Carlson

Ashley R. Carlson grew up wanting a talking animal friend and superpowers and, when that didn't happen, she decided to write them into existence. She lives in Scottsdale, AZ with four (non-talking) pets and one overactive imagination. She owns Utopia Editing & Ghostwriting Services, a company that makes editing, content creation and marketing fun and enjoyable for any need. Her award-winning steampunk-fantasy novel series, *The Charismatics,* can be found at The Poisoned Pen, on Amazon and at her website.

Rebecca Carter

Rebecca got her start working with parasols after being asked to help paint a few 'Kaylee' style parasols for the *Can't Stop the Serenity* charity screenings benefiting Equality Now and Kids Need To Read. She has donated over fifty parasols in the last ten years.

Craig W. Chenery

Craig W. Chenery is a British born author and screenwriter with a particular interest in the zombie, horror, comedy, pop culture, *Star Wars* and special effects genres. Chenery is also an artist, songwriter, voice over actor and improviser.

Connie Cockrell

A 20-year Air Force career, a manager at a computer operations company, wife, mother, sister and volunteer, provides a rich background for Connie Cockrell's story-telling. She writes about whatever comes into her head so her books could be in any genre. She's published sixteen books, has been included in five anthologies and been published on EveryDayStories.com and FrontierTales.com. Connie's always on the lookout for a good story idea. Beware, you may be the next one.

Joshua Cruz

Joshua Cruz is a PhD student at Arizona State University studying education. As an avid gamer, he is also interested in how video games might speak to educational, social, and philosophical theories. In his spare time, Josh is a circus performer, capoista and Dance Dance Revolutionary.

Jenn Czep

The cliché is real; the small town girl moved to the big city and made her dreams come true. Writer, adventurer, pirate, bellydancer and crazy cat lady, Czep sword fights with The DREAD Fleet pirates, cavorts with the beautiful bellydancers of bint Hazine, and enjoys the company of troublesome trolls, magical mermaids, and pesky pixies.

Ryan Dalton

Ryan Dalton is author of the young adult *Time Shift Trilogy*. His debut novel, *The Year of Lightning*, was released January 2016, and its sequel, *The Black Tempest*, in April 2017. Ryan splits his time between writing books during the day, fighting crime at night and hanging out in his awesome underground lair. Please do not tell anyone he's Batman. It's a secret.

Michael D'Ambrosio

Michael is a resident of the Philadelphia area who participates in conventions across the country. Besides writing sci-fi novels for thirteen years, he has also taken up screenwriting and is adapting his novels to script form. A retired member of the USAF/Air National Guard, Michael currently works at a nuclear generating station in New Jersey. Traveling around the world has fed his creativity for writing, which started in the Middle East in the nineties. Phoenix is like a second home to Michael and coincidentally is where he participated in his first convention: Westercon 2004 at the Wigwam Resort.

Bruce Davis

Bruce Davis is a Mesa-based general and trauma surgeon. He finished medical school at the University of Illinois College of Medicine in Chicago in the 1970s and did his surgical residency at Bethesda Naval Hospital. After 14 years on active duty that included duty with the Seabees, time on large gray boats and a tour with the Marines during the First Gulf War, he went into private practice near Phoenix. He is part of that dying breed of dinosaurs, the solo general surgeon. His nonfiction memoir, *Dancing in the Operating Room*, is a glimpse into the life and training of a trauma surgeon.

He also writes science fiction and fantasy novels. His independently published works include the YA novel, *Queen Mab Courtesy*; his military science fiction novel *That Which Is Human*; and the *Profit Logbook* series, *Glowgems for Profit*, *Thieves Profit* and *Profit and Loss*. *Platinum Magic* is his first foray into the world of fantasy, and his first novel with Brick Cave. It represents the start of an exciting new series set in a surprising modern world, like our own, only different.

Emily Devenport

Nine of Emily Devenport's novels have been published in the U.S. by NAL/Penguin/Roc, under three pen names (the others are Maggy Thomas and Lee Hogan): *Shade*, *Larissa*, *Scorpianne*, *EggHeads*, *The Kronos Condition*, *GodHeads*, *Broken Time* (which was nominated for the Philip K. Dick Award) *Belarus* and *Enemies*. She has also been published in the U.K., Italy and Israel. Her ebooks, *The Night Shifters* and *Spirits of Glory* are available from Amazon, Smashwords, etc. She has two new novels forthcoming from Tor: *Medusa Uploaded* and an untitled sequel. Her short stories have been published in *Asimov's Science Fiction*, the *Full Spectrum* anthology, *The Mammoth Book of Kaiju*, *Uncanny*, *Cicada*, *Science Fiction World*, *Clarkesworld* and *Aboriginal SF*, whose readers voted her a Boomerang Award.

J. L. Doty

Jim Doty is a full-time SF&F writer, scientist (with a Ph.D. in Electrical Engineering), laser geek and former running-dog-lackey for the bourgeois capitalist establishment. He's been writing for over thirty years, with ten published books. Four years ago, his self-published books went word-of-mouth viral and sold enough that he was able to quit his day-job, start working for himself and write full time. That led to contracts with traditional publishers and his books are now a mix of traditional and self-published.

His tenth novel, the third in his urban fantasy series, *The Dead Among Us*, was released in February of 2017. Right now, he's pitching his eleventh novel, *The Witch of Val d'Ossa*, to publishers; he's fleshing out ideas for the next book in *The Dead Among Us*; he's working on a new military SF series, *The Blacksword Regiment*; and he's writing another episode in *The Treasons Cycle*. Science is a passion, but writing is an addiction.

Craig L. Dyer

Craig Dyer came to Arizona from New York in the mid '70s. Through a twist of fate, he became involved in the Society for Creative Anachronism where he is known as Lord Craig of the White Cliffs. From the SCA it was a short trip to fannish activities. On Saturday evenings at conventions he can usually be found accompanied by several large, white, wooden ammunition chests, in which he keeps a generous supply of homemade vodka-based cordials. He combines the spirit of a vintner with the showmanship of a low-key P. T. Barnum, as he joyfully discusses the ingredients and watches the pleasure on the faces of his (new and long-held) fannish friends.

Fannishly, he has chaired CopperCon 19 (1999), HexaCon 10 (2000) and HexaCon 12 (2002) as well as ConKopelli, the 2004 Westercon. Additionally he was the webmaster for the Central Arizona Speculative Fiction Society (CASFS) from 1998 to 2011 and is a past keeper of the database and co-editor of *ConNotations* for CASFS. Craig is a founding member and current board chair of the WesternSFA.

Jonathan Elliott

Jonathan Hayes Franklin Elliott is a security systems coordinator by day and alcohol aficionado by night, who only uses his full name when he's trying to be pretentious and sound important. As an Aries and ENTP, he's typically very competitive; however, his +10 charisma often fools people into finding him charming. He's a wanderer at heart and would love nothing better than leaving to travel the world at a moment's notice.

Marcus Fields

Marcus Macabre is a self proclaimed horror punk and musician. He has a working knowledge of modern and classic horror ranging from *Nosferatu* to Creepy Pastas.

Crystel Flanders

From having a vast knife collection to bathing in the blood of virgins, Crystel lives a life that dwells in the inner recesses of horror. Catch her on a good day and she'll smile at you; catch her on a bad day and she'll still smile at you, but only while she's slowly disemboweling you with a rusty spoon. She also likes puppies, kittens and shit like that.

Dirk Folmer

Professor Theodoric Brandywine has been involved with steampunk for a decade and has been a practitioner of bartitsu for nearly as long. The Professor is also a fencing master and a student of Danse de Rue Savate. He has developed a following of dedicated Moustachioed Brothers, and is producing a line of Gentlemen's Grooming products. He is particularly noted for his all natural moustache wax and will be giving a panel on how to make it. As he says, "Not all makers are prop builders."

Janie Franz

Janie Franz comes from a long line of liars and storytellers with roots deep in east Tennessee. Honed by the frigid Northern Plains and the high desert of New Mexico, as well as a degree in anthropology, her writing skill and curiosity generated thousands of feature and cover articles over a vast range of topics for hundreds of regional, national, and international publications before retiring. She co-wrote two books with Texas wedding DJ, Bill Cox (*The Ultimate Wedding Ceremony Book* and *The Ultimate Wedding Reception Book*), and self-published a writing manual, *Freelance Writing: It's a Business, Stupid!*

After telling other people's stories, Janie Franz wanted to tell her own, publishing eleven digital titles with MuseItUp. She is the author of a six-part fantasy series in two sections: *The Bowdancer Saga*, now in print, and *The Lost Song Trilogy*, due in paperback this year. *Discovery* and *Artifacts* kick off her anthropology romance thriller trilogy, *Ruins*; she's working on the third, *Legacy*. Her contemporaries, *Sugar Magnolia* and *The Premier*, offer readers a glimpse into the music industry, for which she was a music journalist, and Hollywood.

Mark Greenawalt

This will be Mark Greenawalt's third Westercon presenting a live body painting demonstration. He is a local resident of Phoenix and dabbles in many art forms including photography, music, writing and lighting design, but he is best known for his artwork on living canvas. His book,

Coats of Paint, is a soft cover portfolio of his body art images compiled from projects around the globe.

Cat Greenberg

Cat Greenberg is a writer and singer/songwriter from St. Louis, MO. She is a founding member of the filk band The Unusual Suspects along with her daughter, Valerie Ritchie, and Mark Ewbank (and of whom Cat's late husband, Bari Greenberg, was an integral part).

Her fiction has appeared in *Marion Zimmer Bradley's Fantasy Magazine*, the DAW anthologies *Sword & Sorceress 11* and *Four Moons of Darkover* (under former name Sandra C. Morrese) and in *Sword & Sorceress 29* with a story co-authored with Bari. She also has a non-fiction book out, *Evolving Understanding*. She spent fourteen years as the advertising director for *The Bulletin of the Science Fiction & Fantasy Writers of America* and was the Public Relations Chair for Archon, the St. Louis area SF convention, for three years.

In 2012, she and Bari together opened Mountain Cat Media LLC, producing their band's debut CD, Accidental Filk Band, and in 2013 the couple's duet CD, Romancing the Filk. Since her husband's death, Cat has expanded the company to include publishing. She also writes the blog An Ordinary Feminist for the company's website.

Vaughan Grey

Vaughan Grey is a host of Shuddercast, a podcast review show of features that can be found on horror streaming service, shudder.com.

Justin Hackert

Justin Hackert of Hackert Helmets and Props has been part of the cosplay community for over 10 years, with a focus on EVA foam armor and helmets.

Paul Haidinger

Paul Haidinger produces amazing costumes and props through Frank and Nat's Armory with his equally talented wife, Debra. He's been building costumes for seven years and loves David Bowie (the singer and dog).

Francis Hamit

Hamit is a long-time fan and this will be his 113th science fiction con. Francis has made a life-long study of Intelligence and Security, once worked for a branch of the National Security Agency and has a MFA in Fiction from the Iowa Writers Workshop. He is the author of several works of historical fiction about spies and spying. He lives in Los Angeles.

Jamie Hanrahan

Professional hardcore geek. Also, K6UHI. Will debug BSODs for food.

Keith Henson

Keith Henson, BSEE UofAZ 1969 was one of the L5 Society founders (1975). He has worked on power satellites off and on for forty years, intensively since he retired. He has written widely on space engineering topics, such as space farms, vapor phase fabrication, large scale radiator designs, power satellites and space transportation systems, recently electric propulsion powered by microwaves.

Ernest Hogan

Ernest Hogan's novels *Cortez on Jupiter*, *High Aztech* and *Smoking Mirror Blues* have earned him the reputation of being the Father of Chicano Science Fiction. He been published in *Amazing Stories*, *Analog*, *Science Fiction Eye* and *Aztlan*. His latest stories are in *Latin@ Rising*, *Five to the Future*, *Mithila Review* and *The Jewish Mexican Literary Review*. *The Terrible Twelves*, a collaboration with his wife, Emily Devenport, is on Tapastic.

Jose Ho-Guanipa

Jose Ho-Guanipa is a host of Shuddercast, a podcast review show of features that can be found on horror streaming service, shudder.com.

Arlys Holloway

Arlys Holloway was raised in Glendale, Arizona, when it still had a small-town western feel. She hails from a long line of women named Arlys, including her mother and daughter. She created the character Ione D. for Facebook posts promoting Vaughn Treude's novel *Fidelio's Automata*, but the character took on a life of her own. Arlys is the co-author of *Miss Ione D. and the Mayan Marvel* and *Professor Ione D. and the Epicurean Incident*. Arlys and Vaughn also created the play *One Good Man*, a comedy about on-line dating, which is appropriate since that is how they met.

H. Paul Honsinger

H. Paul Honsinger is proud to have recently completed Step 5 A (iii)(g) (2), Paragraph 4(s) of "12 Steps for Recovering Attorneys" and now writes full time. Paul is the author of the *Man of War* science fiction trilogy, consisting of novels *To Honor You Call Us*, *For Honor We Stand* and *Brothers in Valor*. The follow up novel, *To Stations My Lads*, due in 2018, continues the story into a new trilogy. Paul's novels are epic space combat tales, in the vein of the Age of Sail novels of Patrick O'Brian and C. S. Forester.

Mark Horning

Mark Horning entered fandom by jumping straight into the deep end: his first con was the 1993 Worldcon, where he was promptly led astray by filkers. A singer-songwriter, physicist and folk musician originally from California, he moved to Arizona in 1996. Mark has degrees in Physics from Cal Poly, San Luis Obispo and Arizona State, and works in the aerospace and defense industry when not out playing his 6 and 12 string guitars.

Dr. Steven D. Howe

Steve Howe is a nuclear scientist and science fiction author/fan. In 2015 he stepped down as the Director of the Center for Space Nuclear Research (CSNR) at the Idaho National Laboratory in Idaho Falls, ID. The CSNR is pursuing development of a radioisotope powered Mars Hopper, nuclear rockets, and advanced power sources for human exploration. Prior to this, he worked at the Los Alamos National Laboratory for twenty years in areas such as nuclear weapons physics, nuclear rockets, in-situ resource utilization for space exploration, manned-Mars missions, medium-energy particle physics, antimatter physics, and fusion/plasma physics. As part of these efforts, he flew on the KC-135 "vomit comet", poked his nose in the hatch of the space shuttle Atlantis while it sat on the pad, created a large hole in the ground at the Nevada Test Site, and had various other fun experiences. Steve has also co-founded a company, Hbar Technologies LLC, to commercialize the use of antimatter. Currently, he works for Dr. Troy Howe at Howe Industries LLC in Tempe, AZ.

In addition to his regular activities, Dr. Howe is a published author of fiction having published the novella, "Wrench and Claw", in *Analog*. He also published the novel, *Honor Bound Honor Born*, which detailed the possible development of the first commercial base on the Moon. In addition to over fifty technical papers published worldwide and his published fiction works, he has also appeared in numerous television programs about space and rocketry.

Khurt Khave

Khurt Khave is a prolific author, steampunk philanderer and the head priest of the First United Church of Cthulhu.

Samantha Kitts

Samantha Kitts founded Thermocosplay in 2014. Since then Sam has striven to explore the materials, techniques and tools used for cosplay crafting. Thermocosplay is now a three person team which works towards entertaining and educating the world on all things cosplay.

Eric T. Knight

Eric T. Knight grew up on a working cattle ranch in the Arizona desert in the '60s and '70s. If you're thinking that sounds romantic, let him stop you right there! Replace those thoughts of 10-gallon hats and six-shooters with old, rusted trucks; sagging barbed-wire fences; sway-backed horses and unending work. Which probably has a lot to do with why he became a writer. It involves more sitting than ranching does, though most of the time the pay has been the same. He says, "I've been writing novels for almost 30 years and it's possible some of them are even worth reading."

Bridget Landry

Bridget Landry was educated as a chemist and planetary scientist, trained as an engineer and has worked in spacecraft operations for more than 25 years. She has worked on the Hubble Space Telescope, the joint US-French oceanographic Earth-orbiter Topex, the (wildly successful!) Mars Pathfinder project, the Cassini mission to Saturn, the Dawn mission at the asteroid Vesta and the Mars Reconnaissance Orbiter. Currently, she is on the sequencing team for Mars Odyssey, which has done relay work for the MER rovers, the Phoenix lander and Curiosity, while returning data on the Martian surface and atmosphere.

Ms. Landry also takes great interest in the advancement of women in technical fields, and the helps and bars to their progress, as well as in the problem of sparking and maintaining girls' early interest in STEM fields. In her technical hat, she has been on science-related panels at Worldcons, local and regional conventions.

Ms. Landry has been an active fan since the age of 13, when she worked for four hours at her first SF con before ever getting her badge. She is a Master-level costumer with a twisted sense of humor, most noted for the Strauss Waltz Assault Team, Computer Pirates, and the Victorian Bathing Beauties. She has won both presentation and workmanship awards, and participated in costuming panels and workshops up to Worldcon levels.

Suzanne Lazear

Suzanne Lazear writes books that end in 'punk'. Book one of her elfpunk series, *The Secret Lives of Rockstars*, is out now with part two releasing this summer. She is also the author of the fairytale steampunk series, *The Aether Chronicles*. Suzanne lives in Southern California with her daughter and the hubby where she's currently attempting to make a raygun to match her ballgown.

Bob Leeper

Bob Leeper is the co-owner and manager of "Arizona's Pop Culture and Alternative Art Network", Evermore Nevermore. He is the co-creator of the pop culture events Steampunk Street and Encredicon and is a member of the Phoenix Film Critics Society. He also curates the Facebook fan site 'The Arizona Cave - AZ Fans of Edgar Rice Burroughs', and is one of the few brave and bold fans of Jar Jar Binks.

Tom Leveen

Tom Leveen is the author of eight novels with imprints of Random House, Simon & Schuster and Abrams. He has also teamed up with Todd McFarlane writing *Spawn*, the comic book series, and released two indie books: a how-to guide for writers on the subject of dialogue and a horror novella based on real events. Currently an early literacy specialist with Phoenix Public Library, he also has 22 years of theater experience as an actor/director and has been Artistic Director at two theater companies.

Jacqueline Lichtenberg

Jacqueline Lichtenberg is a professional reviewer, editor, the creator of the Sime~Gen Universe, the primary author of *Star Trek Lives!*, the founder of the *Star Trek* Welcommittee, creator of the term 'Intimate Adventure', winner of the Galaxy Award for Spirituality in Science Fiction and the first *Romantic Times* Award for Best Science Fiction Novel. Her work is available in e-book, print, audiobook and dramatization on Satellite Radio. She has new novels due in 2017 and *Sime~Gen* is being developed for a video game.

Syd Logsdon

Syd Logsdon has been a carpenter, cabinet maker, surgical tech, Red Cross director and school teacher (of 27 years). And a writer. He has two BSs and two MAs for the love of learning, as well as a teaching credential as writing doesn't pay the rent. Early on, Syd had a novella in *Galaxy* and novels from Ballantine and Pocket Books; one was published in German translation. Then came a dry spell when things stopped selling. Now Syd is back in print with his new novel *Cyan*, out from EDGE since April.

Jeffrey J. Mariotte

Jeff Mariotte is the award-winning author of more than sixty novels, including thrillers *Empty Rooms* and *The Devil's Bait*; supernatural thrillers *Season of the Wolf*, *Missing White Girl*, *River Runs Red* and *Cold Black Hearts*; horror epic *The Slab*; the *Dark Vengeance* teen horror quartet and others. With his partner and wife Marsheila Rockwell, he wrote the science fiction/horror/thriller *7 Sykos* and has published numerous shorter works.

He also writes comics, including the long-running horror/western series *Desperadoes* and original graphic novels *Zombie Cop* and *Fade to Black.* He has worked in virtually every aspect of the book business and is currently the division chief of Visionary Books.

Tristan Marshall

Tristan was a boy scout, centerfielder, soldier, sailor, singer, soccer coach, the retail management end of several big corporations, a member of five National Slam Teams, a couple of State Teams and once a Comic Con Nerd Slam champion. He is father, son, husband, brother, journeyman laminator (yeah, I made that up), painter/artist, reluctant teacher, mentor and occasional muse. He has been working on a book of poetry since the relative "dawn of time" (don't hold your breath), but things like work, painting, reading, sleep, lack (or excess) of ego, open mics, music, binge watching British crime dramas and a million of other excuses, stymies this endeavor as much as his four fingered typing.

Jen McAlonan

Jen is a member of the West Coast Nerd Corps podcast, as well as a local educator and musician. Of particular interest is educating young adults on gender disparities and homosocial overtones inherent in late-Victorian adventure fiction and scientific romances (as per the standard curriculum of English Composition). Of course, she'll educate any "willing" participant about gender disparities and homosocial overtones inherent in just about anything they try to enjoy. She also writes stuff that's... well, just awful.

Chris McLennan

Chris McLennan loves horror movies. Chris McLennan loves film festivals. After attending many festivals over a long period of time, Chris, with a tiny dream and a ton of marketing experience thought it would be fun to have a festival of their own. FearCON started out as a tiny film festival (Phoenix Fear Film Festival) at an even tinier Art Gallery, which has blossomed into the Phoenix FearCON Horror Film Festival and Convention, run by Chris and Jim McLennan.

Cathy McManamon

Cathy McManamon is a life-long Chicagoan who has played music since childhood. Guitar is her first love, but she also plays hand and electronic kit drum and can fake her way through keyboards. She dabbles with renaissance instruments and music when no one else is listening. Cathy grew up playing in church where she learned to write, arrange and direct a choir. She survived ten years teaching elementary general music classes. Cathy is now part of the folk/rock group Random Fractions (formerly Three-Fifths) and the hard rock/filk band Toyboat. She runs a monthly drum circle and is a ritual drummer/facilitator for the pagan community.

Ernesto Moncado

Born and raised in Mexico City, Ernesto Moncado has been a Phoenix resident since the beginning of the 21st century. He is a visual artist, a published novelist and poet; a playwright, actor and stage director; a stand-up comedian and MC; a sideshow and stilt performer; and a percussion enthusiast. Since 2008, he produces and hosts variety shows and open mic events like *Firestage*, and leads the Arcana Collective, an experimental theater troupe. He also founded Los Subtítulos, the only bilingual improv troupe in Arizona, with members of The Torch Theatre, Arturo Ruíz and Xchel Hernández.

Yvonne Navarro

Yvonne Navarro lives in southern Arizona and is the author of twenty-three published novels and over a hundred short stories, plus numerous non-fiction articles and two editions of a reference dictionary. Her writing has won the HWA's Bram Stoker Award plus a number of other writing awards. She also draws and paints and once sold a canvas print of a zombie painting. She is married to author Weston Ochse and dotes on their rescued Great Danes, Ghoulie, The Grimmy Beast and I Am Groot. They also have a talking, people-loving parakeet named BirdZilla. Her most recent work of fiction is *Supernatural: The Usual Sacrifices* (based in the *Supernatural* Universe). She is currently working on 4,273 projects. Okay, maybe it just feels that way. All the time.

Bob Nelson

Bob Nelson is the chief of Brick Cave Media, a media microglomerate for the crazy ideas that he dreams up, including Brick Cave Books. He serves on the board of Anthology, Inc, is an avid fan and supporter of poetry and a lover of all things kaiju.

Amy K. Nichols

Amy K. Nichols has been a musician, web designer, political assistant, teacher and armchair scientist. She's traveled overseas, studied medieval paleography, learned how to weld, been complimented by Benedict Cumberbatch and survived being crushed by drunken Scots. She lives in Peoria with her husband, two children and many books. She's the author of the YA science fiction novels *Now That You're Here* and *While You Were Gone*, published by Knopf. She currently teaches writing with the Your Novel Year program at ASU and is plotting her next adventure.

Brian Olnick

Brian is a member of the West Coast Nerd Corps podcast. An avid fan of video games and comics, he has been a gamer as far back as he can remember. Being raised by *Nicktoons* and platformers has given him a lifetime of experiences that he enjoys sharing with others.

Open Beta

Open Beta is an eclectic group with roots in traditional folk and modern Irish music, while also delving into filk and nerd/rock. The band members have each played in other projects and have been entertaining crowds and building momentum in this project for a little over two years. With Brian drumming, Erin fiddling, Paul... guitaring (yes, it's a word) and all three lending vocals to music inspired by *Star Wars*, *Firefly* and *Lord of the Rings*, they deliver energetic performances that will have you singing along.

Katie Panveno

Katie is a rainbow K-Pop warrior who showers under the eternal spigot of tomato sauce. She enjoys the little things in life, such as dressing in all black, hissing at small children and not smiling.

Alyssa Provan

Alyssa is a rainbow K-pop warrior who showers under the eternal spigot of tomato sauce. Her turn-ons include short men with large, hairy feet, an inclination towards magic and death scenes exclusively featuring Sean Bean. Her turn-offs include mean people and giant towers with large, glowing eyes that probably spy on people while they're showering.

Deena Remiel

Deena spends her time playing in the Garden of Good and Evil as she writes fantasy, paranormal romance and suspense. She's been known to down beers with her angels and even put Satan in his place. She enjoys playing with the concept of immortality and all its implications. She and her family live in Gilbert, AZ, near her beloved Superstition Mountains.

Frankie Robertson

Frankie Robertson writes romantic fiction with an otherworldly twist. She is the author of the romantic fantasy series, *Vinlanders' Saga;* the urban fantasy/paranormal romance series, *Celestial Affairs*; and *Veiled Mirror*, a stand-alone paranormal mystery. As a reader, her first love was sf/f; then discovered romance so she blends elements of both. With a background in real estate, occupational therapy and paranormal investigation, she brings a diverse experience to her stories. Frankie's most recent release is *Guardian*, the second book in the *Celestial Affairs* series.

Marsheila Rockwell

Multiple Scribe and Rhysling Award nominee Marcy Rockwell is the author of eleven books and is currently working on the twelfth (with husband/writing partner Jeffrey J. Mariotte), a novel based on the popular video game Mafia III. Her work includes the acclaimed horror/SF novel *7 Sykos* and a *Xena: Warrior Princess* trilogy (both with Mariotte); the *Shard Axe* series, the only official novels for the global MMORPG, Dungeons & Dragons Online; two collections; dozens of short stories and poems; and articles on writing and the writing process. She has also served as a mentor for Arizona State University's Your Novel Year program.

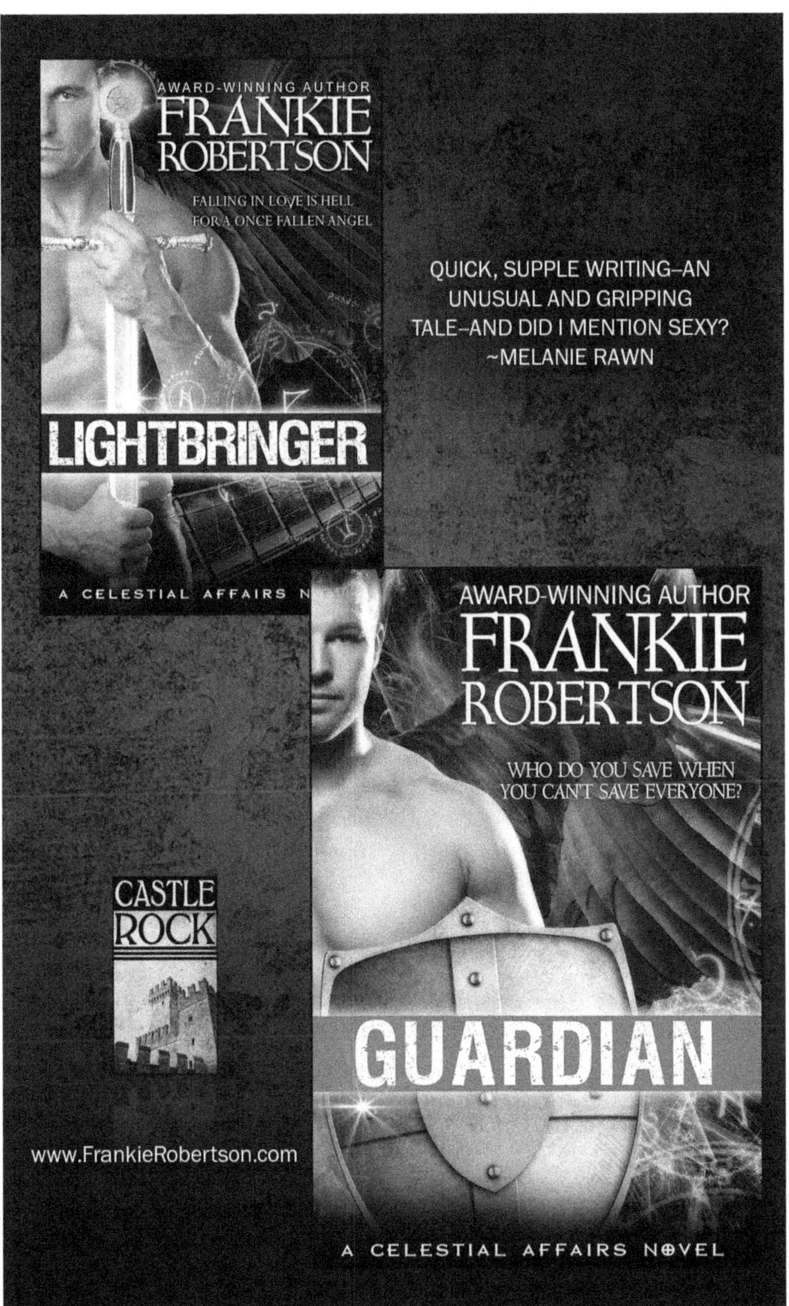
AWARD-WINNING AUTHOR
FRANKIE
ROBERTSON
FALLING IN LOVE IS HELL
FOR A ONCE FALLEN ANGEL
LIGHTBRINGER
A CELESTIAL AFFAIRS N
QUICK, SUPPLE WRITING--AN
UNUSUAL AND GRIPPING
TALE--AND DID I MENTION SEXY?
~MELANIE RAWN
AWARD-WINNING AUTHOR
FRANKIE
ROBERTSON
WHO DO YOU SAVE WHEN
YOU CAN'T SAVE EVERYONE?
CASTLE
ROCK
GUARDIAN
www.FrankieRobertson.com
A CELESTIAL AFFAIRS NOVEL

Annette Sexton-Ruiz

Annette Sexton-Ruiz was born in Chicago and has lived most of her life in Arizona. She has studied art in Puerto Rico, Italy, England, Ireland and Cuba and she has a Bachelors in Art History from ASU; her work has been displayed nationally and internationally. She participated in the Chicano Art Movement in Chicago's "Little Mexico" in the '80s and Self-Help Graphics in East Los Angeles throughout the '90s. She has worked in three different Phoenix museums over fifteen years and has been a curator of art exhibitions in the east LA Chicano art scene and San Francisco's Mission Cultural Center. She has participated in local sci-fi fandom since the mid '90s with participation in art programming.

Sharon Skinner

Sharon Skinner holds a BA in English, an MA in Creative Writing and a poetic license. She writes in the fantasy, steampunk and paranormal genres. Her latest Young Adult novel, *Collars and Curses* (Brick Cave Books), is a coming-of-age urban fantasy about navigating relationships and high school as a shapeshifting teenager. She is a regular presenter and panelist at various writing conferences and book festivals, and makes appearances at a variety of ComiCons and pop culture conventions. Sharon currently serves as the Regional Advisor for the Society of Children's Book Writers and Illustrators for the Arizona region.

T. L. Smith

T. L. Smith was born in Louisiana, but calls Phoenix, AZ home between bouts of wanderlust. Even a stint in the U.S. Air Force as a radar specialist brought her back to the desert. Her time in the service taught her to appreciate military and social cultures and ever-changing technologies, giving life to the science fictions she loves so much.

Kellie Springer

Kellie Springer has been a member of the steampunk community for the past six years. She is an active member in the Tucson Steampunk Society. While a great fan of the many genres of geek culture, the fashion, gadgets and creativity of steampunk won her heart. She can often be seen decked out in Victoriana and properly chapeau'd. A former champion of tea duelling and a veteran teapot racer, she enjoys all manner of diversions.

Kevin Standlee

Kevin Standlee was co-Chair of the 2002 Worldcon. He is a director of SFSFC, Inc. (1993, 2002, and 2018 Worldcons; and 2000, 2011, and 2013 Westercons) and of CanSMOF (2009 Worldcon) and he is currently Chair of the WSFS Mark Protection Committee. Kevin's first SF convention was the 1984 Worldcon, and he has worked on conventions in roles from gopher to Worldcon Chairman. Kevin is an expert on the rules of Worldcon and Westercon.

His other hobbies include trains and rail transit. Kevin is a computer programmer for a supply-chain management company, dividing his time between an office in the Bay Area and his home in Fernley, Nevada.

Katherine Stewart

Katherine Stewart, known as "Bustle Girl" in the cosplay world, is an actor, writer, director and costume designer with a couple of decades in the arts world. As the founder and artistic director of Desert Rose Theatre, Katherine directed approximately thirty plays with a special emphasis on Shakespeare and the classics. Recently she directed and appeared in a film adaptation of *Two Gentlemen of Verona*. Her experience on stage and in film has given her a unique perspective which she's used in workshops and seminars. She is often seen around the local convention scene as a panelist and cosplayer. She also is an event emcee, seen most recently on several occasions with Scottsdale Public Art.

Katherine encourages interaction at events, and usually has treats for small children. On social media, Bustle Girl describes herself as "costumer, cosplayer and candy giver."

Edward Sulfaro

Ed is a lifelong fan of sci-fi, fantasy and everything in between. Particular interests include urban fantasy, urbane sci-fi, hyphen fictions such as -punk and cyber-, magical realism, graphic novels, indie webcomics, podcasts, the self-contained story arc, side quests, open world video games, mixed virtual reality and commas. Especially commas. Currently, he is the sound editor on the Humorless Rants podcast, a political show discussing current national news with an unapologetic liberal perspective.

David Lee Summers

David Lee Summers is the author of ten novels, along with numerous short stories and poems. His writing spans a wide range of the imaginative from science fiction to fantasy to horror. His most recent novels are *The Astronomer's Crypt*; and *The Brazen Shark*, which won the Preditors & Editors Reader's Choice Award for best steampunk novel of 2016. His short stories and poems have appeared in such magazines and anthologies as *Realms of Fantasy*, *Cemetery Dance* and *Straight Outta Tombstone*. He's been nominated twice for the Science Fiction Poetry Association's Rhysling Award. When not writing, David operates telescopes at Kitt Peak National Observatory.

Chris Swanson

Chris Swanson is a writer, blogger and general smart-guy who flatters himself by believing the world cares what he has to say.

Vaughn Treude

Vaughn Treude grew up on a farm in North Dakota and has been reading science fiction and fantasy as long as he can remember. In 2012, he published his first novel, *Centrifugal Force*, about computer hackers who overthrow the U.S. government. Since then he has concentrated on steampunk, writing *Fidelio's Automata* and co-authoring the *Professor Ione D.* series of young adult novels with his wife Arlys Holloway. Vaughn and Arlys are also co-creators of the musical comedy *One Good Man*, which is loosely based on Arlys's experiences in the on-line dating world.

Jet Veridis

Jet is a teenage magician who has been performing professionally for private and public events in the Valley of the Sun since 2014. He specializes in close-up magic and walk around magic for parties and corporate events.

Julie K. Verley

Julie K. Verley, otherwise known as Tabitha Bradley, is an established e-book author, DAZ Studio creator and fan of crochet. With a background in writing and costuming and a healthy interest in animation, Julie joins Westercon 70 in the hopes of sharing her enthusiasm for creating with all attendees. Her latest book, *Once in a Blue Moon*, is available on Amazon.

Cynthia Ward

Cynthia Ward has published stories in *Asimov's Science Fiction*, *Shattered Prism*, *Weird Tales*, *Athena's Daughters* and other anthologies and magazines. She edited the anthologies *Lost Trails: Forgotten Tales of the Weird West Volumes One and Two* for WolfSinger Publications. With Nisi Shawl, Cynthia co-created the groundbreaking *Writing the Other* fiction writers workshop and coauthored the diversity fiction-writing handbook *Writing the Other: A Practical Approach* (Aqueduct Press). Her short novel, *The Adventure of the Incognita Countess*, was released earlier this year by Aqueduct Press. She lives in Los Angeles, where she is not working on a screenplay.

Thomas Watson

Thomas Watson is a Tucson based writer and author of the five part *War of the Second Iteration* series: *The Luck of Han'anga*, *Founders' Effect*, *The Plight of the Eli'ahtna*, *The Courage to Accept* and *Setha'im Prosh*. An unrelated science fiction novel, working title *The Ironwing Affair*, is currently under construction and should be available later this year. Among his other interests, he's an amateur astronomer and has published a short memoir, *Mr. Olcott's Skies: An Old Book and a Youthful Obsession*, that explores his relationship with the night sky. He currently works at the Steward Observatory as a property coordinator.

Stephanie Weippert

Stephanie is bibliophile — full stop. Leave her alone for ten minutes and she will be reading or writing. Stephanie is married and claims she and her husband are naturally insane in a fun and harmless way. Together they do filking and other musical hobbies. Their teen boys often drive them toward the not-fun insanity (Nature or Nurture? - you decide). With former careers as a legal assistant and a licensed massage therapist, she now gets to make writing a full time endeavor thanks to her awesome husband.

Lee Whiteside

Lee Whiteside is the webmaster of SFTV.org, which has been keeping track of science fiction and fantasy TV schedules and news since the early 1990s. He's heavily involved with Arizona science fiction and fantasy cons. Chair for three, he's also filled way too many committee positions.

Austin Wright

Austin Wright is a fan of science fiction. He has presented panels in ten different states. When not attending conventions, he is trying to visit every country in the world.

Natalie Wright

Natalie is the author of the award-winning science fiction series *H.A.L.F.* and *The Akasha Chronicles*, a popular young adult fantasy trilogy with over two million reads on Wattpad. She lives in Tucson, AZ with her husband, teen daughter and two cat overlords. Natalie spends her time writing, reading, geeking out over nerd culture and cool science, meeting readers and fans at book festivals and comic cons throughout the western United States. Natalie appears frequently on podcasts and vlogs for book lovers and geeks such as The Speculative Fiction Cantina, Front Row Geeks and iHeart Radio.

Jamie Wyman

As an author, Jamie's favorite playgrounds are urban fantasy, horror and creepy carnival settings. She has published an urban fantasy series, *Etudes in C#*, which follows a technomage through a Las Vegas full of gambling trickster gods and mayhem. She has had the pleasure of writing alternate universe Sherlock Holmes stories for Abaddon Books, which put the Great Detective in the setting of a Depression-era American circus. Jamie is also a freelance editor and a contributor for Cracked.com.

Ben Yalow

Ben has been to about 800 conventions and worked on several hundred of them, at levels ranging from gofer to chair of several regionals and Worldcon Division Head and Chair staff. He's also edited four books for NESFA Press, two of which were nominated for the Hugo Award (for which he says credit should go to the author's material, not his editing).

Timothy Yamamura

Timothy Yamamura is a new faculty member in the English department at Northern Arizona University, where he teach classes on post-colonial, transnational and world literatures. His research and teaching interests include transnational Asian American literary studies, post-colonialism in Asia/Pacific, science fiction studies and critical race, ethnic, diaspora, and cultural studies.

A San Francisco-native, he graduated with honors with a B.A. in English from Seattle University, earned two M.A.'s in Professional Writing and East Asian Languages and Cultures from the University of Southern California, and recently completed my PhD in Literature at UC Santa Cruz. He has an essay, "Fictions of Science, American Orientalism, and the Alien/Asian of Percival Lowell," in a forthcoming collection on the representation of Asia in science fiction, *Bamboo Worlds*, published by the University Press of Mississippi.

Misako Yamazaki

Misako Yamazaki is a college student majoring in English/creative writing. She spends her free time reading, writing and doing anything nerdy. Her fandoms include but are not limited to *Harry Potter/Fantastic Beasts*, *Supernatural* and anime (e. g., *Yuri!!! On Ice*). She self-published a book of her poetry and dreams of becoming a bestselling author.

Panelist Websites

Here are the websites of our panelists and participants.

Acoustically Sound	acoustically-sound.net
Linda D. Addison	cith.org/linda
Allen Amis	allenamis.com
Anabel Amis	facebook.com/anabelamisart
Madame Askew	madameaskew.com
Hal C. F. Astell	apocalypselaterempire.com
Kim Bailey	kimbailey.com
Colette Black	coletteblack.net
Nathan Blackwell	squishystudios.com
Maya Bohnhoff	mayabohnhoff.com
Ashley Carlson	ashleyrcarlson.com
Craig W. Chenery	craigwchenery.com
Connie Cockrell	conniesrandomthoughts.com
Ryan Dalton	ryandaltonwrites.com
Michael D'Ambrosio	fracturedtime.com
Bruce Davis	thatwhichishuman.com
Emily Devenport	emsjoiedeweird.com
J. L. Doty	jldoty.com
Jason Drotman	wildwestcon.com
Janie Franz	janiefranz.fourfour.com
Mark Greenawalt	markgreenawalt.com
Justin Hackert	facebook.com/hackerthelmets
Ernest Hogan	mondoernesto.com
H. Paul Honsinger	hpaulhonsinger.com
Khurt Khave	chainsawalice.blogspot.com
Eric T. Knight	erictknight.wordpress.com
Suzanne Lazear	suzannewrites.blogspot.com
Bob Leeper	evermorenevermore.com
Tom Leveen	tomleveen.com

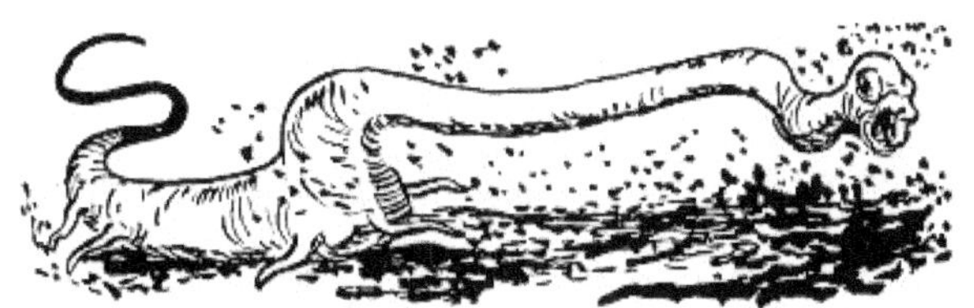

Jacqueline Lichtenberg	simegen.com/jl
Syd Logsdon	sydlogsdon.com
Jeffrey J. Mariotte	jeffmariotte.com
Chris McLennan	trashcity.com
Cathy McManamon	facebook.com/cathymcmusic
Jim Miller	crithitaz.com
Yvonne Navarro	yvonnenavarro.com
Bob Nelson	brickcavemedia.com
Amy K. Nichols	amyknichols.com
Open Beta	openbetamusic.com
Deena Remiel	deenaremiel.com
Frankie Robertson	frankierobertson.wordpress.com
Marsheila Rockwell	marsheilarockwell.com
Annette Sexton-Ruiz	annettesextonruiz.teamdroid.com
Sharon Skinner	sharonskinner.com
T. L. Smith	tlsmithauthor.com
Kevin Standlee	kevin-standlee.livejournal.com
David Lee Summers	davidleesummers.com
Vaughn Treude	vaughntreude.com
Jet Veridis	facebook.com/jetveridis
Julie K. Verley	diranda.com
Cynthia Ward	cynthiaward.com
Thomas Watson	facebook.com/thomas.watson
Stephanie Weippert	stephanieweippert.com
Natalie Wright	nataliewrightauthor.com
Jamie Wyman	housepajamazon.com
Ben Yalow	panix.com/~ybmcu
Jason Youngdale	maricopacon.com

Panel Programming

Art

Art Auction

Monday, 4.00pm-5.00pm - Cloister

Artwork displayed for auction that receives three or more written bids by the end of the Art Show will go to voice auction. The Art Auction is when this happens. Bid in the Art Show and bid higher at the Auction!

Artists' Reception

Sunday, 5.00pm-7.00pm - Palm B/C - Displaying Artists

Come celebrate the artists who are displaying their work in our Art Show at an Artists' Reception, which will be hosted in our Art Show with courtesy snacks and a cash bar.

The Art of Julie Dillon

Monday 11.00am-12.00pm - Dolores - Julie Dillon

Julie Dillon gives a presentation of the artwork that she has created (and won awards with) over the years.

Body Painting with Mark Greenawalt

Saturday 7.00pm-11.00pm - Dolores - Mark Greenawalt

Mark Greenawalt's live body painting demo will breathe life into a brand new original character. Model Griffin Maria will be transformed into the Hollow Queen from the new storyline from Todd VanHooser called *Wheelhouse*.

Cover Art: The Visual Allure of a Book

Saturday 12.30pm-1.30pm - Xavier - Anabel Amis, Julie Dillon, Larry Elmore

Hear from our artists' perspective on how to make a visually captivating and enticing book cover.

Creating a Coloring Book

Sunday 12.30pm-1.30pm - Jokake - Gilead, Stella Miller

What goes into creating your own coloring book? Gilead has created a few and will show you what it takes.

Digital Art Using DAZ Studio

Saturday 12:00pm-1:00pm - Capistrano - Julie K. Verley

Using the free program, DAZ Studio, you can create beautiful artwork just like Poser, without the investment. Learn how from Arizona DAZ artist Julie K. Verley.

Digital Painting with Julie Dillon

Monday 12.30pm-1.30pm - Cavetto - Julie Dillon

Julie Dillon breaks down her digital painting process, showing step by step how her art is made.

Draw the Figure

Monday 5.00pm-6.00pm - Campanile - Gilead, Stella Miller

Join acclaimed local artist, Gilead, for a demonstration on the art of drawing the human figure.

From Concept to Reality: Digital Art Painting

Tuesday 12.30pm-1.30pm - Campanile - Anabel Amis

Fantasy and sci-fi concept artist Anabel Amis covers her tips and tricks for digital painting in Photoshop, as well as where to find expanded resources to help you bring your own artwork to the next level. This panel will feature a new book cover sample for *The War Bard.*

Introduction to Crochet for Amigurumi (Beginner's Crochet)

Sunday 9:30am-10:30am - Cavetto - Julie K. Verley

In this panel, we will look at the Japanese art of Amigurumi and learn a few basic stitches. Then we will use those stitches to make an amulet bag! Some supplies will be provided, but feel free to bring your own.

Paper Mache 101

Monday 2.00pm-3.00pm - Campanile - Tom Deadstuff

Join our Local Artist GoH, Tom Deadstuff, for a talk about the basics of the art of paper mache.

Sketch Off

Sunday 9.30am-10.30am - Palm E/F - Anabel Amis, Gilead, Larry Elmore

We supply the artists, you ("the audience") supply the themes. The artists have ten minutes to sketch it. They'll do this for three sketches each, then the art will be auctioned at the end of the event.

Spotlight on Larry Elmore

Tuesday 12.30pm-1.30pm - Palm E/F - Larry Elmore

We shine a spotlight on our Special Artist Guest of Honor, Larry Elmore, kindly sponsored by LepreCon 44.

What to Draw When There's Nothing to Draw?

Tuesday 2.00pm-3.00pm - Jokake - Julie Dillon, Tom Deadstuff, Larry Elmore, Gilead

This panel aims to answer that unanswerable, time-honored question: "Where do ideas come from?"

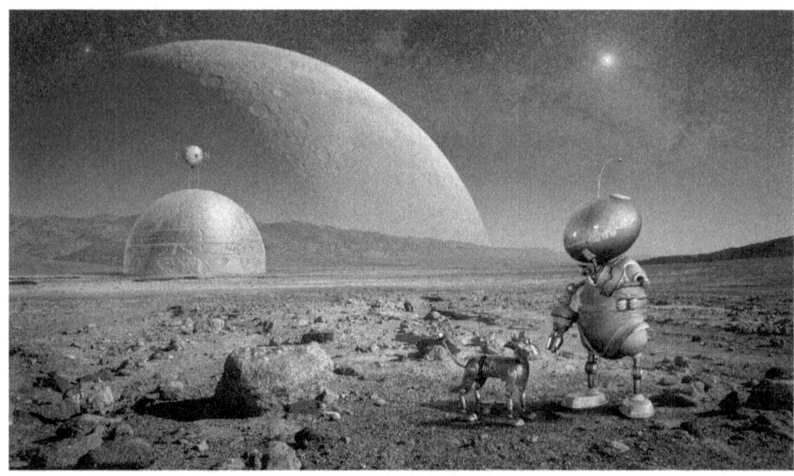

Books and Authors

19th Century Science Fiction

Sunday 2.00pm-3.00pm - Jokake - Paige Walters, Austin Wright

A look at obscure work from notorious authors such as Mary Shelley, Nathaniel Hawthorne, H. G. Wells, Jules Verne and others!

Alien Autopsy: The Biology of E.T.

Sunday 5.00pm-6.00pm - Dolores - Bruce Davis, Jacqueline Lichtenberg, Syd Logsdon, David Lee Summers, Thomas Watson

Would it be possible for an alien species which found water poisonous to even land on Earth? How would two hearts work? What does green Vulcan blood say about their circulatory system? Join our scientific experts and authors as they get to the guts of creature creation and make sure that “damned alien biology” is more than just a vague explanation.

Beyond Gold and Silver: The Dawn of a New Age in Sci-Fi

Monday 2.00pm-3.00pm - Jokake - Colette Black, Connie Cockrell, Michael D’Ambrosio, H. Paul Honsinger, Jacqueline Lichtenberg

Calling all geeks and nerds - welcome to your promised land! In the last few years, we’ve seen a resurgence of “serious” sci-fi films such as *Gravity*, *Interstellar*, *The Martian* and *Arrival* and upcoming *Ready Player One*. The *Star Trek* franchise is thriving and *Star Wars* is back on the big screen (though some argue it’s fantasy, not sci-fi, but hey, space ships...) Mars One is looking for volunteers. We’re fascinated by technology, futurism, space, final frontiers and as always, the examination of the nature of existence and human culture, societies and institutions. Science fiction is where it’s at! Join a discussion of the sci-fi renaissance and why it’s happening now.

Build a Story Live (Workshop)

Monday 11.00am-12.00pm - Ironstone - Ashley Carlson, Ryan Dalton, Janie Franz, Eric T. Knight, Tom Leveen

Join YA author Ryan Dalton and his team of authors for this live exercise in creativity. You provide the prompts, they’ll supply the story.

Bullets in Space: Putting the "Sci" in Sci-Fi

Tuesday 9.30am-10.30am - Campanile - Michael D'Ambrosio, Steve Howe, Amy K. Nichols, David Lee Summers, Thomas Watson

Hard sci-fi requires intensive research and lots of math to make sure everything adds up. We talk about that process, where to find the scientific answers and how to make sure your story doesn't get bogged down in physics calculations.

Classics of Science Fiction: The Sword of Rhiannon

Sunday 12.30pm-1.30pm - Boardroom - John Hertz

Discussion of *The Sword of Rhiannon* by Leigh Brackett. It's been called her best early work; concise, eloquent, fresh, poetic. "Why a sword?" is answered, also "Is this science fiction?" Perhaps unanswerable by human beings, but addressed, are questions of identity, motive, recognition and will, during an adventure in our great romantic tradition.

Classics of Science Fiction: The Lights in the Sky are Stars

Sunday 11.00am-12.00pm - Boardroom - John Hertz

Discussion of *The Lights in the Sky are Stars* by Fredric Brown. Some say this belonged on the Retrospective Hugo ballot at Noreascon IV (62nd World Science Fiction Convention) – and argue over which it should have replaced, *The Caves of Steel*, *Childhood's End*, *Fahrenheit 451*, *Mission of Gravity*, or *More Than Human*. A straightforward s-f novel by Brown - and what a wallop!

Classics of Science Fiction: The Time Machine

Sunday 10.30am-11.30pm - Boardroom - John Hertz

Discussion of *The Time Machine* by H. G. Wells. Far better known in the wide wide world than our other two – why? Never mind marketing; Hesse's *Glass Bead Game* won the Nobel Prize in Literature. In fact we see only two distant times: the more gripping is narrated in a way which, upon reflection, is quite suspect. And the Time Traveller never returns for lunch.

Doorways and Devices: Accessing Magical/Alternative Realms

Tuesday 12.30pm-1.30pm - Xavier - Michael D'Ambrosio, Janie Franz, Amy K. Nichols, Frankie Robertson, Connie Willis

Whether using a time machine, a rip in reality or a ring of standing stones, new adventures await willing (and sometimes unwilling) travelers on the other side of these portals. Our panel examines the timeless trope.

Dystopias: Despots or Desolation?

Saturday 2.00pm-3.00pm - Dolores - Bruce Davis, Gini Koch, Amy K. Nichols, Weston Ochse, Natalie Wright

Call it zeitgeist, but dystopias are all the rage. For now. Our panelists look at the appeal of the bleak future, and whether the current state of the world might spur more optimistic stories.

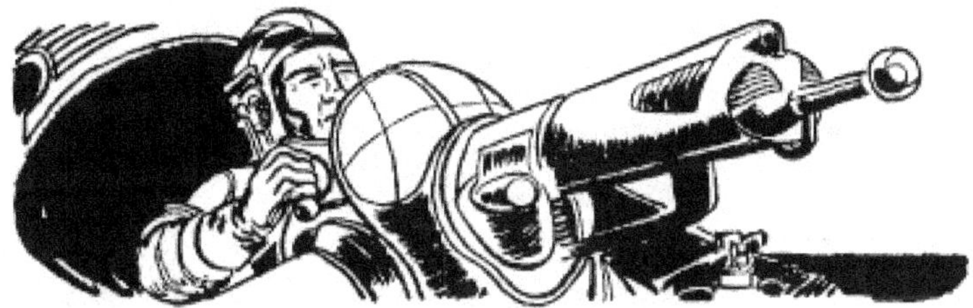

Electronic Books for Sci-Fi and Fantasy Lovers

Monday 11.00am-12.00pm - Cavetto - Julie K. Verley

Introduction to electronic/digital publishing for readers. Introduces you to the wide world of electronic fiction available online, including places to find it and ways to enjoy it.

Fake It Till You Make It: A Survivor's Guide for the Introverted Author

Saturday 12.30am-1.30pm - Dolores - Janie Franz, Gini Koch, Amy K. Nichols, T. L. Smith, Jamie Wyman

Every successful modern-day author makes public appearances, whether for signings, conferences or cons. No matter how much you might want to hide behind your book cover, eventually you'll have to step into the spotlight and meet your fans. This panel will discuss tips and tricks to engage your readers with enthusiasm and authenticity.

The Fate of the Horror Anthology

Saturday 7.00pm-8.00pm - Campanile - Jonathan Elliott, Marcus Fields, Crystel Flanders

In America, short horror stories gained momentum in the mid-20th century through a variety of media. We will revisit various incarnations of horror anthologies, before exploring their current trend in traditional comics, film and television and transformation into something else.

The Female Hero's Journey: Strong Women in Sci-Fi/Fantasy

12.30pm-1.30pm - Dolores - Gini Koch, Yvonne Navarro, Marsheila Rockwell, Cynthia Ward, Jamie Wyman

With critics, fans and feminists alike heralding the arrival of the *Wonder Woman* movie, is there a new age of badass female heroes coming? We look at what makes a badass female hero, and select our old favorites.

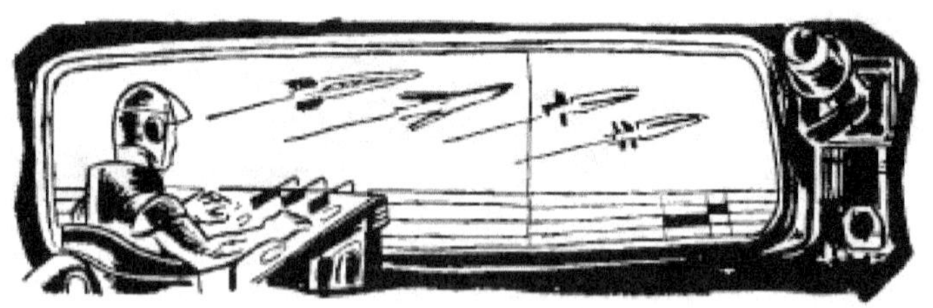

Fight Me! Writing Effective Fight Scenes

Saturday 3.30pm-4.30pm - Cavetto - Maya Bohnhoff, Jenn Czep

Buckle your swash with pirate Jenn Czep as she teaches you how to make your blades dance with flair, while still keeping the story flowing.

From Pen to Press: Navigating Your Book to Publication (Workshop)

Sunday 2.00pm-3.00pm - Ironstone - Janie Franz, Deena Remiel

You've turned your great idea into the next masterpiece. Now what? Deena Remiel helps you navigate the process of finding agents and selling your novel, or how to self-publish.

Girls with Guns: Writing Women into Your Action Scenes (Workshop)

Sunday 2.00pm-3.00pm - Palm E/F - Jenn Czep, Gini Koch, Suzanne Lazear, T. L. Smith, Jamie Wyman

This is the 21st century, honest! Today's books and movies take female characters beyond the "damsel in distress". Even if she's not your main character, take away the magnolias and give her a magnum or weapon of choice. The panelists will be discussing how to avoid cliché characters and how to embrace them as well. The evolution of female in books and movies is one worth discussing.

Jackalopes and Other Cryptids

Sunday 3.30pm-4.30pm - Sand Lotus - Ernest Hogan, Weston Ochse, David Lee Summers, Thomas Watson

In honor of our mascot, our authors pay tribute to the strange creatures that may or may not inhabit the dark corners of the world.

Killing Your Darlings: Objective Editing Your Own Work

Sunday 11.00am-12.00pm - Ironstone - Sharon Skinner

Sometimes the hardest part of writing is knowing when you have to take a scalpel to your manuscript. Sharon Skinner explains how to let go.

Married With Deadlines: Balancing Home Life When Your Significant Other Also Writes

Sunday 12.30pm-1.30pm - Dolores - Emily Devenport, Ernest Hogan, Jeffrey J. Mariotte, Yvonne Navarro, Marsheila Rockwell, Weston Ochse

Three pairs of husband-and-wife writers share their stories.

Meet and Greet: Connie Willis

Sunday 3.30pm-4.30pm - Boardroom - Connie Willis

Meet our Author GoH, Connie Willis, for a small scale meet and greet.

Meet and Greet: Gini Koch

Tuesday 12.30pm-1.30pm - Boardroom - Gini Koch

Meet our Local Author GoH, Gini Koch, for a small scale meet and greet.

Meet and Greet: Weston Ochse

Sunday 11.00am-12.00pm - Boardroom - Weston Ochse

Meet our Toastmaster, Weston Ochse, for a small scale meet and greet in the Boardroom.

Military Sci-Fi: Getting the Details Right

Saturday 12.30pm-1.30pm - Cloister - H. Paul Honsinger, Weston Ochse, Thomas Watson

Guns, cars and horses... mess up some tiny detail and you will get eviscerated by your readers. This is even more true for military sci-fi. Our panelists discuss the resources to make sure your weapons are accurate and your chain of command doesn't have any broken links.

Of Wizards, Dragons and Klingons: SF/F World Building

Tuesday 11.00am-12.00pm - Jokake - J. L. Doty, Sandra Greenberg, H. Paul Honsinger, Suzanne Lazear, Syd Logsdon

Every movie, television, game and book franchise is built upon the creation of a fictional world. The success of the franchise often depends on how richly the world is imagined. Creation of new languages (or parts of languages), building societies, exploring political systems and the development of religions, sci-fi and fantasy writers are the masters of "What if?" Join a discussion of your favorite fantasy worlds such as *Harry Potter*, the Marvel Universe, *Lord of the Rings, Wheel of Time, Fallout 4, Dragon Age* and others that exemplify the rich world-building we love in our favorite sci-fi and fantasy franchises. The authors on the panel will also share how they create their own fictional worlds.

Planting or Building: Understanding the Pre-Writing Process (Workshop)

Tuesday 11.00am-12.00pm - Ironstone - Deena Remiel

Plotter or pantser? Architect or gardener? Deena Remiel helps you get started on your writer's journey, examining the work you do before the pen hits the paper.

Playing in Somebody Else's Sandbox: Writing Tie-In Fiction

Monday 11.00am-12.00pm - Jokake - Maya Bohnhoff, Jacqueline Lichtenberg, Jeffrey J. Mariotte, Yvonne Navarro, Marsheila Rockwell

Video games, TV shows and films. Their well-developed universes have spawned a wealth of literature, which have in turn influenced the original universe. How can you be creative with someone else's creations, and how do you make your ideas last within the confines of an existing universe.

The Return of the Space Opera

Saturday 3.30pm-4.30pm - Jokake - Colette Black, Michael D'Ambrosio, H. Paul Honsinger, David Lee Summers

With the return of *Star Wars*, the success of *The Expanse* on TV and Pierce Brown's *Red Rising*, the space opera has returned. Our panelists look at the appeal of these action-filled adventures where the science doesn't get too hard and the characters have plenty of drama and romance.

Science and Technology vs. Magic

Monday 9.30am-10.30am - Campanile - Colette Black, Eric T. Knight, Syd Logsdon, David Lee Summers, Thomas Watson

What makes this such a compelling trope?

The Science of Steampunk: What Makes the Gears Go Round?

Sunday 9.30am-10.30am - Jokake - Ashley Carlson, Bruce Davis, Steve Howe, Suzanne Lazear, David Lee Summers

Steampunk style is filled with all sorts of clockwork creatures and fantastical machines. Our scientists and authors look at the science and tech behind airships, submarines and giant mechanical spiders.

Size Matters: Novels vs. Short Stories

Sunday 11.00am-12.00pm - Xavier - Linda D. Addison, Emily Devenport, Sandra Greenberg, Cynthia Ward, Connie Willis

Some stories require ten 1,000-page volumes. Others only need 10,000 words. Our panel discusses how to tell the difference, when to cut your story short and when it needs to grow further.

Space: The Diverse Frontier

Tuesday 3.30pm-4.30pm - Campanile - Linda D. Addison, Ernest Hogan, Jamie Wyman

Star Trek broke ground in the 60s, challenging the social norms on diversity. In recent years, the Hugos have been dominated by women and people of color, but the growing diversity has sparked a backlash. What is the sci-fi community getting right, and where does it still have to boldly go where no-one has gone before?

Spotlight on Connie Willis

Sunday 12.30pm-1.30pm - Palm E/F - Connie Willis

We shine a spotlight on our Author GoH, Connie Willis, who is kindly sponsored by the WesternSFA.

Spotlight on Gini Koch

Monday 3.30pm-4.30pm - Xavier - Gini Koch

We shine a spotlight on our Local Author GoH, Gini Koch.

Spotlight on Weston Ochse

Tuesday 2.00pm-3.00pm - Xavier - Weston Ochse

We shine a spotlight on our Toastmaster, Weston Ochse.

Time Out to Kiss: Romance When the Bullets are Flying

Monday 2.00pm-3.00pm - Ironstone - Ashley Carlson, Frankie Robertson, T. L. Smith, Natalie Wright, Jamie Wyman

For some fans of sci-fi and fantasy, nothing makes the eyes roll more than the protagonist taking a time out to make out while the zombies are busting down the door or the bullets are flying overhead. "The world is ending but you're kissing?!" Yet without the build up of romantic tension and growth and deepening of relationships between the characters, a story may feel flat and flit from one action scene to another without much of interest to hold it together. How do writers of books, film, TV and comics infuse the right amount of relationship building and romantic tension without losing the reader to an eye roll? We'll discuss stories that do it well and explore how it's done.

Vampires and Zombies and Werewolves, Oh My!

Monday 5.00pm-6.00pm - Dolores - Linda D. Addison, Yvonne Navarro, Weston Ochse, Sharon Skinner

Monsters are still around, but in the modern age they've changed - vampires sparkle and zombies run. Can the classic portrayals still summon a scare? What are some of the best new takes on legendary creatures?

Weird, Wild, Urban and Unknown: Speculative Fiction in the Southwest

Monday 12.30pm-1.30pm - Xavier - Suzanne Lazear, Tom Leveen, Amy K. Nichols, Weston Ochse, Connie Willis

The Sonoran Desert has given birth to some classic horror, sci-fi and fantasy, from dystopian cities run by the Humane Society to alternate universes where Phoenix has beachfront property. Our panelists discuss their favorite supernatural Arizona stories, as well as their own.

What No One Tells You About Publishing (Until It's Too Late) (Workshop)

Monday 3.30pm-4.30pm - Ironstone - Tom Leveen

Want the unvarnished, brutal facts about publishing fiction? Grit your teeth and get ready for a program with author Tom Leveen, who unpacks the highs and lows of the publishing world. Tip #1: the moment you decide to make money writing fiction, you've just started a small business.

What Made the Golden Age Golden?

Saturday 2.00pm-3.00pm - Xavier - Connie Cookrell, H. Paul Honsinger, Syd Logsdon, Connie Willis

Heinlein and Asimov are two pillars of the Golden Age of Sci-Fi. But reading those works with modern eyes can reveal attitudes that would be unacceptable in modern times. What can we learn from the classics when we look past the sexist and racist attitudes that pervaded the works of that time? Can we still appreciate works that present unacceptable ideologies?

What's Your Genre?

Monday 5.00pm-6.00pm - Xavier - Colette Black, Connie Cockrell, Frankie Robertson, T. L. Smith, Connie Willis

Peeling the label off books, movies and the authors who write them. Our panel will be looking at who's really behind today's popular fiction and how they mix the genre to draw in wider audiences.

Why So Serious? Humor in Sci-Fi

Tuesday 2.00pm-3.00pm - Palm E/F - Maya Bohnhoff, Ernest Hogan, Gini Koch, Connie Willis, Jamie Wyman

Comic sci-fi and fantasy didn't die with Douglas Adams and Terry Pratchett. Westercon is blessed with a pair of guests who are among the funniest sci-fi writers around. They talk about their favorites and share their secrets in how to keep the mood light amidst death, chaos and scientific explanations.

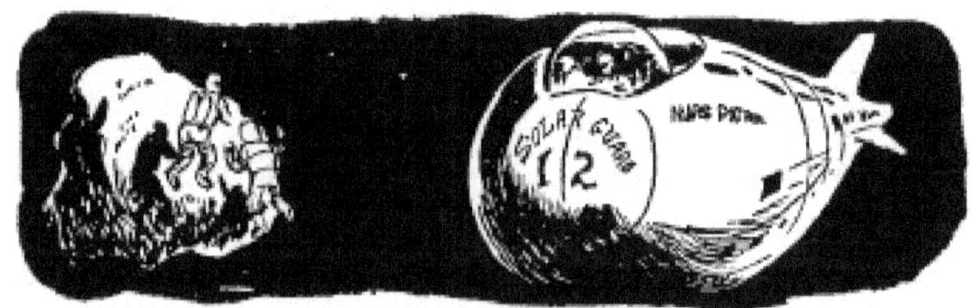

Writing Exceptional Dialogue (Workshop)

Sunday 3.30pm-4.30pm - Cavetto - Tom Leveen

Tom Leveen, author of several novels with imprints of Random House and Simon & Schuster, brings 22 years of theater background to this fast-paced class on how to make your dialogue shine, whether it's for fiction, creative nonfiction, comic scripts or the screen. Bring your notebook!

Writing for Different Media (Workshop)

Sunday 5.00pm-6.00pm - Jokake - Michael D'Ambrosio, Tom Leveen, Jeffrey J. Mariotte

Novels aren't screenplays aren't comic book strips. Our panelists discuss the differences and how to transition from one to another.

Writing Realistic Injuries (Workshop)

Tuesday 11.00am-12.00pm - Campanile - Bruce Davis

Yeah, that wound sounds cool on paper, but would it kill the victim instantly? Trauma surgeon and author, Dr. Bruce Davis, looks at on often overlooked aspect: making sure the gory details are medically possible.

WTF is Branding? How to Sell Yourself

Tuesday 3.30pm-4.30pm - Cavetto - Janie Franz, Deena Remiel, T. L. Smith, Stephanie Weippert

We're told we need a brand, but what is it? Author discuss the challenges with coming up with a brand to identify themselves to the readers. Then getting that brand out to the right venues, like blogs, articles and conferences.

YA That Shines (But Doesn't Sparkle)

Saturday 5.00pm-6.00pm - Jokake - Colette Black, Ashley Carlson, Ryan Dalton, Amy K. Nichols, Natalie Wright

We've all heard the complaints. Teenage love triangles. Werewolves and vampires. And always sparkling, sparkling sparkling! But YA is more than glowing emo undead. Our YA authors challenge the perceptions of the genre and spotlight stories that stand out.

You Must Choose Wisely: Indie vs. Traditional

Saturday 5.00pm-6.00pm - Cavetto - Emily Devenport, J. L. Doty, Deena Remiel, Thomas Watson, Stephanie Weippert

With the advent of self-publishing, writers have more choices than ever to release their book into the wild. But is self-publishing the way to go, or does traditional publishing still have the advantage? Perhaps you want to do something in between, or explore a small press. Our panelists discuss the pros and cons of each route.

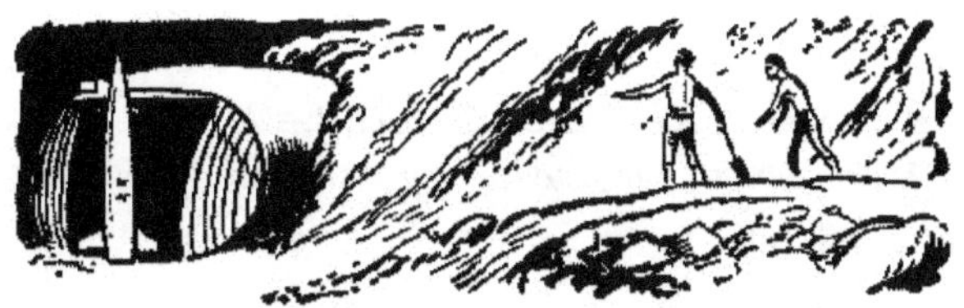

Diversity

Are They Token?

Tuesday 12.30pm-1.30pm - Ironstone - Sandy Manning, Annette Sexton-Ruiz

Talking about diversity characters in comics, TV, movies, etc., looking at whether those characters are there because they're necessary to the story, or just there to fill a diversity quota.

Classic Science Fiction vs. The Modern Perspective

Saturday 12.30pm-1.30pm - Ironstone - Sandy Manning, Jen McAlonan, Edward Sulfaro

It's no secret that classic science fiction has some outdated views on race, gender, sexuality, etc. But is it still possible to enjoy these books in spite of our modern sensibilities? How do we deal with this clash?

Feminism in Doctor Who

Sunday 5.00pm-6.00pm - Ironstone - Crystel Flanders, Sandy Manning, Brian Olnick, Chris Swanson

Older gentleman seeks young, female companion for adventures? An examination of the Companions and how they represent (or fail to represent) the "modern woman".

Sex Positivity and Modern Media

Sunday 7.00pm-8.00pm - Ironstone - Jen McAlonan, Edward Sulfaro

At what point does sexualization become objectification?

Shifting Standards: It's Not Appropriate to Do That Any More

Monday 9.30am-10.30am - Ironstone - Jen McAlonan

Society has evolved in a great many ways, but it seems impossible to avoid offending someone these days. How do we make our way through the minefield of "PC Culture"?

Social Issues in Science Fiction and Fantasy

Saturday 2.00pm-3.00pm - Ironstone - Jen McAlonan, Brian Olnick, Annette Sexton-Ruiz, Edward Sulfaro

How to bring modern issues and viewpoints (LGBT, feminism, poverty, mental illness, immigration, etc.) into science fiction and fantasy literature and media.

Take My Word for It: "No"

Saturday 3.30pm-4.30pm - Ironstone - Jen McAlonan, Brian Olnick

We've all heard the phrase, "Cosplay is not consent." But at what point does "social awkwardness" become harassment? How can you clearly communicate your desire to be left alone without "causing a scene"? What can conventions do to create a safe, fun environment for all?

Women and Gaming

Saturday 5.00pm-6.00pm - Ironstone - Jen McAlonan, Brian Olnick

Do women have different expectations for the games they play than men? Are their experiences any different when playing online? What about streaming game play?

Women in Science

Sunday 12.30pm-1.30pm - Ironstone - Tia Bly, Bridget Landry

Do women in STEM fields face different difficulties than their male counterparts? How can we encourage more young women and girls to enter these fields?

You Betrayed the Law! Law Enforcement and Science Fiction

Sunday 3.30pm-4.30pm - Ironstone - Edward Sulfaro

The police have been portrayed in the media a number of times: *Judge Dredd*, *Minority Report*, *RoboCop*, etc. Where are the police headed? Judges? Pre-crime? Or something more positive?

You Can't Say That (Now)!

Monday 12.30pm-1.30pm - Ironstone - Jen McAlonan

There are a number of words that have fallen out of favor. Let's talk about self-identification labels, labels from other groups, and why certain groups can't say certain words.

Education

Adventures in the Classroom: Using RPGs in Youth Settings

Sunday 4.30pm-5.30pm - Capistrano - Todd VanHooser

Another story telling game is the Role Playing Game (RPG). Join game designer Todd VanHooser for a discussion of using RPGs with youth.

Catapult!

Monday 3.00pm-4.00pm - Capistrano - Tim Griffin

Join GriffinEd founder and Guest of Honor, Tim Griffin, in a workshop on building catapults with kids.

Bang a Drum: Using a Drum Circle to Empower Youth

Monday 1.30pm-2.30pm - Capistrano - Jenn Czep

Join teaching artist and author Jenn Czep on a journey into drumming and how it can be used in after school programs.

From Sir Arthur to Jules Verne: Using Classic Science Fiction and Fantasy in Youth Programming

Sunday 9.00am-10.00am - Capistrano - KellyAnn Bonnell, Jenn Czep

Join Pop Goes the Classroom founder KellyAnn Bonnell and teaching artist Jenn Czep as they discuss ways they have used the classics to create engaging programs for youth.

I Made This!

Monday 12.00pm-1.00pm - Capistrano - TBD

Discover how the maker movement can foster self esteem in youth.

Meet GriffinEd

Monday 9.00am-10.00am - Capistrano - Tim Griffin

People at Westercon have diverse interests and professions. Our Filk GoH, Tim Griffin, is also a youth development professional with amazing resources for youth programs.

More than Monopoly: Using Board Games to Teach Critical Thinking

Sunday 12.00pm-1.00pm - Capistrano - Patricia Stedman

There is a world beyond traditional family games. Learn about what games have to teach and what games work best with different age groups.

STEAM Integration: Using Art and Literature to Build Science Identity

Saturday 1.30pm-2.30pm - Capistrano - KellyAnn Bonnell, Tom Deadstuff

What makes you passionate about science? The stories and images that emerge from art and literature? The explosions and mess? Come join a panel of artists and education experts as they discuss what formed their science identity and how that insight can be used to foster it in youth.

Tell Me a Story: Story Dice/Cards/Stones

Sunday 3.00pm-4.00pm - Capistrano - KellyAnn Bonnell, Jenn Czep

Stories have characters and settings. They have plots with beginnings, middles and endings. Story dice/cards are a unique way to teach these elements to kids in a fun and engaging way. Come learn and play with us.

There's Science in That There Art

Sunday 10.30am-11.30am - Capistrano - Tom Deadstuff

Join Artist GoH Tom Deadstuff and friends as we explore the science in their art and what can be used within youth programs and classrooms.

Using Costuming to Engage Youth

Monday 10.30am-11.30am - Capistrano - TBD

Some affinity groups create their identities with costume. How can this be used in youth programs?

Welcome to Our Affinity Space

Sunday 1.30pm-2.30pm - Capistrano - TBD

Westercon is a place where like minded individuals of all ages can come together and be their uniquely genuine selves. It's an affinity space. Learn about them and how you can use them in your school or youth program.

Where Do We Go from Here?

Monday 4.30pm-5.30pm - Capistrano - KellyAnn Bonnell

Join Pop Goes the Classroom founder KellyAnn Bonnell to discuss realistic ways to incorporate workshop content into your after school program or classroom.

Fandom

Arizona's Early Connections to Popular Culture

Saturday 5.00pm-6.00pm - Xavier - Bob Leeper, Timothy Yamamura

Learn how Edgar Rice Burroughs and Percival Lowell made Arizona the center of the pop culture universe and influenced over a hundred years' worth of comics, books, television shows and films.

Awesomely Awful: Across the Decades

Sunday 7.00pm-8.00pm - Xavier - Hal C. F. Astell, Michael Flanders, Jim Miller

After five years of highly successful panels at Phoenix Comicon, the Awesomelys expand to Westercon 70 to highlight guilty pleasures from a wider range of decades than they're usually able to cover. Join us to see our cinematic picks from the 1950s to the 2000s.

Closing Ceremonies

Tuesday 5.00pm-6.00pm - Palm E/F - Weston Ochse, Guests of Honor

Even though we don't want the con to end, we have to wrap sometime. Join us as Toastmaster Weston Ochse ends Westercon 70 in style and our chair, Dee Astell, literally passes the Westercon gavel on to Nikki Ebright, who will chair Westercon 71 in Westminster, CO this time next year.

Check out Westercon 71 at their fan table, at their parties or online.

Crowdsourcing Conventions

Sunday 3.30pm-4.30pm - Jokake - Chris McLennan, Jim Miller, Jason Youngdale

Everyone knows a crowdsourcing horror story, but it's a valid tool in the conrunner's toolbox. Join three local conrunners who have financed successful multi-year cons (Crit Hit!, MaricopaCon and Phoenix FearCon), through Indiegogo or Kickstarter and learn how they did it.

Fannish Inquisition

Sunday 11.00am-12.00pm - Sand Lotus - Ben Yalow

Everybody expects the Fannish Inquisition! It's a traditional Westercon opportunity for those bidding to host future Westercons (and sometimes Worldcons) to present their bids to anyone who's interested.

Feedback Session

Sand Lotus, Tuesday, 3.30pm-4.30pm - Dee Astell, Hal C. F. Astell

Please tell us (and future Westercon hosts) what we did right or wrong.

Milk Junkies and Velociraptor Love Tabasco: Erotic FanFic from the Depths of the Internet

Sunday 8.30pm-9.30pm - Xavier - Joshua Cruz, Jonathan Elliott, Crystel Flanders, Michael Flanders

Join our panelists as they try their very, very, very hardest to deliver dramatic readings of fan-favorite eroticism from the depths of the internet before inevitably bursting out into sexually-intensified laughter. **Restricted to *18+*.**

How Fandom Has Changed in Half a Century

Sunday 2.00pm-3.00pm - Sand Lotus - Val & Ron Ontell, Bjo & John Trimble

From letter writing campaigns and fanzines through bulletin boards and conventions to the wide open world of the internet, how has fandom changed in half a century and where is it going next?

Meet the Fan Guests of Honor: Val & Ron Ontell

Monday 11.00am-12.00pm - Xavier - Val & Ron Ontell

Join our Fan GoHs, Val & Ron Ontell, for a journey back through their history as prominent fans in New York and San Diego and elsewhere.

Opening Ceremonies

Saturday 4.00pm-5.00pm - Palm E/F - Weston Ochse, Guests of Honor

Westercon 70 officially opens at noon on Saturday, though some things will start earlier. However, our Opening Ceremonies are scheduled for 4.00pm to ensure that everyone who wants to be there can be.

Join our Toastmaster, Weston Ochse, as he introduces all our Guests of Honor and gets the ball officially rolling for Westercon 70.

Running Niche Conventions in a Mainstream World

Tuesday 11.00am-12.00pm - Xavier - Jason Drotman, Diana Given, Chris McLennan, Henry Vanderbilt

In a world where geek culture is mainstream and Comicons attract six figure attendances, how do niche cons survive and even thrive? Join our panelists, who collectively run Phoenix FearCon, Space Access and Wild Wild West Steampunk Convention as they explain.

Westercon Business Meeting

Monday 12.30pm-1.00pm - Sand Lotus - Kevin Standlee, Lisa Hayes

The annual Westercon business meeting, led by Kevin Standlee.

Worldcon Tours: Looking Forward to Helsinki

Tuesday 2.00pm-3.00pm - Cavetto - Val & Ron Ontell

Our Fan Guests of Honor, Val & Ron Ontell, have been running tours in connection with overseas Worldcons since 1987, when Ron was the official travel agent for the Conspiracy. Their past tours have included Britain (twice), Ireland, Japan, and Australia (twice) and yes, they are running one to Scandinavia in 2017. Look back at where they've been and forward at where they're going in the run up to Worldcon in Helsinki in August.

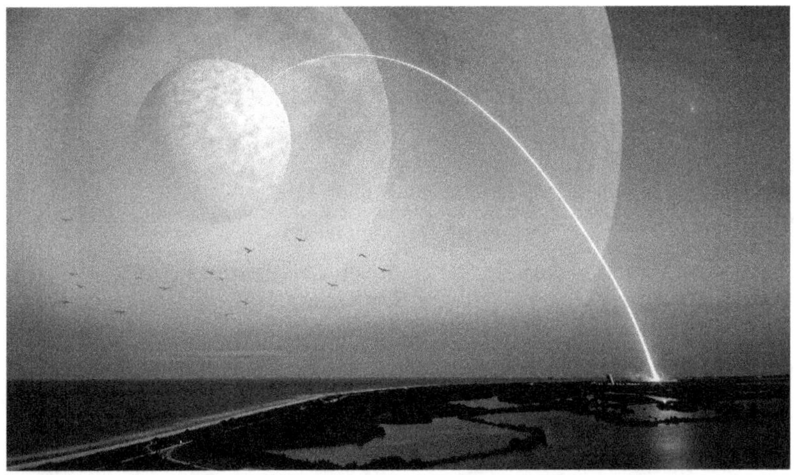

Filk

We've dedicated the Joshua Tree to our Filk programming.

Against the Norm

Tuesday 11.00am-12.00pm - Cavetto - Brian Abernathy, Erin Lewis, Cathy McManamon, Paul Schmidt

Join our filkers to discover how to work a niche band within a cookie-cutter/pop environment.

Beginning Songwriting Workshop

Sunday 11.00am-12.00pm - Dolores - Tim Griffin, Maya Bohnhoff

Come join award-winning songwriter and teacher Tim Griffin as he walks you through the process of turning a cool idea into a complete song. Tim has done this workshop with kindergarteners, octogenarians and everyone in between. Trust me, you can do this! All ages welcome.

Can You Hear Me Now? Microphones and How to Use Them

Saturday, 1.30pm-2.30pm - Joshua Tree - Gerry Tyra

An introduction on how to use the microphone to make the most of your time on stage. Learn how to not make your sound guy hate you.

Dead Dog Filk

Tuesday 2.00pm-4.30pm - Joshua Tree

Wrap up the convention musically with our Dead Dog Filk session.

Drum Circle

Saturday 12.00pm-1.00pm - Joshua Tree - Capt. Ares

Sunday 11.00am-12.00pm - Joshua Tree - Capt. Ares

Monday 11.00am-12.00pm - Joshua Tree - Cathy McManamon

Tuesday 11.00am-12.00pm - Joshua Tree - Capt. Ares

Guitars are Cool, Right?

Saturday 12.30pm-1.30pm - Jokake - Jeff Bohnhoff, Mark Horning, Paul Schmidt

Guitar workshop: tips and tricks from some of our experts.

Hey, I Know That Song! Parody Writing Workshop

Saturday 5.00pm-6.00pm - Joshua Tree - Jeff Bohnhoff, Maya Bohnhoff, Mark Ewbank, Gary Swaty

Parodies: how and why do we write them?

Middle-Eastern Drum Workshop

Monday 9.30am-10.30am - Joshua Tree - Capt. Ares

Interested in learning how the belly dancers' drummers do it? Bring your own drum if you have one.

Open Filk

Joshua Tree, Friday, Saturday, Sunday and Monday 9.00pm-whenever

Come and listen or join in with our open filking sessions.

Recording for Dummies

Sunday 7.00pm-8.00pm - Joshua Tree - Brian Abernethy, Tim Griffin

Learn from the masters how recording music works. We have props!

Filk Concerts

All filk concerts are in Joshua Tree except where marked.

***Tim Griffin* - Saturday 3.00pm-4.00pm - in Palm E/F**

Jeff & Maya Bohnhoff - Monday 7.00pm-8.00pm
Lady Cat - Sunday 5.00pm-5.30pm
Lynn Gold - Sunday 5.30pm-6.00pm
Tim Griffin (children's) - Sunday 2.00pm-3.00pm
Jennifer Horning - Monday 2.00pm-3.00pm
Mark Horning - Monday 12.30pm-1.30pm
Magical Wanderings - Monday 5.00pm-6.00pm
Magic Mark - Sunday 4.00pm-4.30pm
Cathy McManamon - Monday 3.30pm-4.30pm
Open Beta - Sunday 12.30pm-1.30pm
The Unusual Suspects - Saturday 7.00pm-8.00pm
Wandering Storyteller: Damsels in Distress - Sunday 3.30pm-4.00pm

So Many Drums!

Sunday 9.30am-10.30am - Joshua Tree - Brian Abernethy, Capt. Ares, Jen McAlonan, Cathy McManamon

There are so many different types of drums and styles of drumming. Where did they all come from, what are they all for and which is for me?

Theme Filk

Saturday 8.00pm-9.00pm - Joshua Tree - theme is A-Z

Sunday 8.00pm-9.00pm - Joshua Tree - theme is Teaching Songs

Monday 8.00pm-9.00pm - Joshua Tree - theme is Space

Tim Griffin Wants Your Music (And He Pays Royalties)

Tuesday 9.30am-10.30am - Joshua Tree - Tim Griffin

When Tim isn't filking, he runs a nonprofit called GriffinEd that uses fun educational music to help kids learn science, math, history and other great stuff for school. Think *Schoolhouse Rock* and you've got the basic idea. If you've got a good teaching song or if you're just curious, come get the lowdown on how we use music to help kids learn, while making a little money in the process.

Traveling with Instruments: Practicality, Regulations and the Future

Monday 11.00am-12.00pm - Sand Lotus - Mark Horning

Travel with your instruments can be frustrating, especially if you're flying. Increasing regulation of international trade is making it even tougher for overseas travelers. Discuss the practicalities of traveling with your instruments at home and abroad.

The Westercon Song

Tuesday 12.30pm-1.30pm - Joshua Tree - Tim Griffin, Valerie Ritchie

Which of our illustrious filkers can write the most entertaining song about this year's festivities? Come join the fun! There be prizes here!

Film

Apocalypse Later Mini-Film Festival

Friday 7.00pm-8.30pm - Xavier - Hal C. F. Astell of Apocalypse Later

Hal C. F. Astell of Apocalypse Later programs and presents mini-film festivals at conventions across the southwest and this will be event #26. It's his fifth year running at LepreCon and his second Westercon (after two well-received sets at Westercon 68 in San Diego).

At Westercon 70, he'll present a curated 90 minute set of international award-winning science fiction and fantasy short films, some of which you can't see outside the film festival circuit.

At the Movies

Sunday, 12.30pm-2.30pm - Xavier - Len Berger

This is a favorite convention panel at Arizona genre cons. You will get a sneak peak at trailers for some exciting upcoming movies then, after the trailers, we will hold a raffle for *free* movie promotional material (T-shirts, baseball caps, special posters and more). The late Barry Bard started this panel decades ago and we all miss Barry. Sponsored by CASFS (the Central Arizona Speculative Fiction Society).

At the Movies - Indie Style

Tuesday 12.30pm-2.30pm - Wind Flower - Len Berger

This is a new flavor for an old favorite panel at Arizona genre cons. You will get a sneak peak at trailers for some exciting upcoming independent movies that may or may not end up in your local theater. After the trailers we will hold a raffle for *free* movie promotional material (T-shirts, baseball caps, special posters and more). Sponsored by CASFS.

Babylon 5: Discussion and History

Tuesday 2.00pm-3.00pm - Ironstone - Lee Whiteside

Join Lee Whiteside, the webmaster of SFTV.org, which has been keeping track of science fiction and fantasy TV schedules and news since the early 1990s, for an overview of *Babylon 5*.

Behind the Scenes on *Space Above and Beyond*

Saturday 12.30pm-1.30pm - Cavetto - Kim Bailey

Kim Bailey was the Technical Designer on *Space Above and Beyond* for its entire run. Come and learn about the first science fiction show to have a realistic military presence in space and hear about behind the scenes from a first hand perspective.

Kaiju: Just Big Giant Monsters or More?

Sunday 5.00pm-6.00pm - Cavetto - Bob Nelson, David Rybacki

Open discussion on kaiju or giant monsters: past, present and future.

The Making of a Web Series: *Voyage Trekkers* and *Lucidity Web Saga*

Sunday 2.00pm-3.00pm - Dolores - Nathan Blackwell, Craig Curtis, Sean Oliver

The creatives behind *Voyage Trekkers* and *Lucidity Web Saga* will share their secrets on creating popular web series and talk about their recent BluRay release and future plans for *Voyage Trekkers.*

The Making of *Christopher Marlowe*

Saturday 3.30pm-4.30pm - Dolores - Francis Hamit

This is a film about the poet, playwright and spy set in the Elizabethan Era. A brilliant scholar and the best-known playwright of the day until he got killed, Marlowe also worked for the Crown as a spy. Francis Hamit will describe why it takes so long for motion pictures to move from concept to the screen. As the Managing Director of The Kit Marlowe Film Co. plc and an Executive Producer and the screenwriter for *Christopher Marlowe*, a feature film to be made in the UK next year, he has a first-hand knowledge of the process. The film is based upon a stage play he presented in 1988 and turning it into a cinematic product involved multiple rewrites and negotiations with talent, agents, sales agents and production facilities. He will discuss how tax incentives now drive creative choices and how being an Executive Producer involved in the process is the best way to protect the integrity of your work while still getting the film made.

A New World: Creating *Star Trek* Fandom

Tuesday 1.30pm-2.30pm - Capistrano - Bjo & John Trimble, Dr. Dave Williams

In 1966 a new TV show aired unlike any previously seen before. *Star Trek* developed a dedicated fan following from the very beginning. How did this happen? What was Trek fandom like in its very first decade? Join UFP President, Dr. Dave Williams, Bjo and John Trimble and others for a look back to where it all began.

Pop Culture Builds Better Communities

Tuesday 9.30am-10.30am - Cavetto - Craig W. Chenery

Social groups, costuming, conventions, trading trivia and fandom as a business all bring a sense of belonging and bring people together.

Roddenberry vs. Abrams: Two Timelines, Two Visions of *Trek*

Monday 12.30pm-1.30pm - Jokake - Bjo & John Trimble, Dr. Dave Williams

Join a panel of Treksperts including Bjo and John Trimble who will compare and contrast both *Star Treks* for a friendly discussions of how *Star Trek* has changed over the decades.

Sci-Fi Tube Talk

Monday 3.30pm-4.30pm - Cavetto - Lee Whiteside

Join Lee Whiteside, the webmaster of SFTV.org, which has been keeping track of science fiction and fantasy TV schedules and news since the early 1990s, for a runthrough of what's upcoming.

Shuddercast Live Podcast Panel

Monday 9.30am-10.30am - Cavetto - Vaughan Grey, Jose Ho-Guanipa

The podcast hosts will be recording an episode live while discussing a film available on Shuddercast, a streaming horror film service. Film TBD.

Star Trek: Discussion and History

Tuesday 9.30am-10.30pm - Ironstone - Lee Whiteside

Join Lee Whiteside, the webmaster of SFTV.org, which has been keeping track of science fiction and fantasy TV schedules and news since the early 1990s, for an overview of *Star Trek*, past, present and future.

Star Trek: The Original Series: A 50th Anniversary Retrospective

Sunday 5.00pm-6.00pm - Sand Lotus - Bjo & John Trimble, Dr. Dave Williams

This year marks the 50th Anniversary of the broadcast of *Star Trek*'s first season. Join UFP President Dr. David Williams, plus Bjo and John Trimble for this retrospective panel on *The Original Series.*

Star Wars: 40 Year Retrospective

Tuesday 12.30pm-1.30pm - Dolores - Craig W. Chenery

Star Wars has now been known to the public for forty years. Come and learn about the universe and its fandoms and share your experiences.

Still Boldly Going: *Star Trek*'s Continuing Legacy

Tuesday 3.00pm-4.00pm - Capistrano - Bjo & John Trimble, Dr. Dave Williams

Star Trek lives! *Star Trek Discovery* is premiering late summer/early fall and plans are underway for the next movie, building from last summer's *Star Trek Beyond*. There are more *Star Trek* fan films coming out out this year too, as well as much merchandising. Join a panel of Treksperts including Bjo and John Trimble for a discussion of new *Trek* and its future!

Technical Design Elements in Film (*Mission to Mars / Stargate*)

Sunday 9.30am-10.30am - Dolores - Kim Bailey

Technical Designers are the visual artists and storytellers tasked with making the technology and science realistic and based in some reality, in consultation primarily with the director. Learn about and discuss the "How To" of Technical Design by the technical designer behind *Mission to Mars, Stargate* and more.

Working the Art Department from *Blade Runner* to *Mission to Mars* and Beyond

Saturday 2.00pm-3.00pm - Cavetto - Kim Bailey

Production designers are the visual artists and storytellers who, in consultation primarily with the director, create and develop the overall look, atmosphere and emotion that move the story in any film or television project. Learn about and discuss the 'How To' of Art Direction and Production Design.

General

Charity Auction

Monday 1.30pm-2.30pm - Cloister - Jen McAlonan, J. B. Talbott

100% of the proceeds from our Charity Auction will benefit the Challenger Space Center in Peoria, AZ. Come and bid on a wide variety of books, hardcover and paperback, signed and unsigned, along with art proofs, jewelry, movie memorabilia, space posters and more. Charity Auction Program Guides will be available at Registration, listing all items under the hammer and details are also online.

The Center of Attention: Exploring the Aesthetic of Surveillance in the Horror Video Game

Sunday 3.00pm-4.00pm - Campanile - Joshua Cruz, Michael Flanders

Drawing heavily from the *Silent Hill* franchise (as well as *Outlast*, the recent *Resident Evil 7*, and *Psychonauts*), we show how video games are in a prime position to use an "aesthetic of surveillance" to create feelings of uncertainty, discomfort, dis-ease and terror. We provide examples of ways game developers create the sense of "being watched" to contribute to the atmosphere of games and suggest that an aesthetic of surveillance should be of immediate consideration for those working in the horror genre.

Dead Dog

Tuesday 6.00pm-whenever - ConSuite

You don't have to go home but you can't stay here! Well, actually you can. If you're not involved in taking down the event, then sit back and relax with new friends and old in the ConSuite.

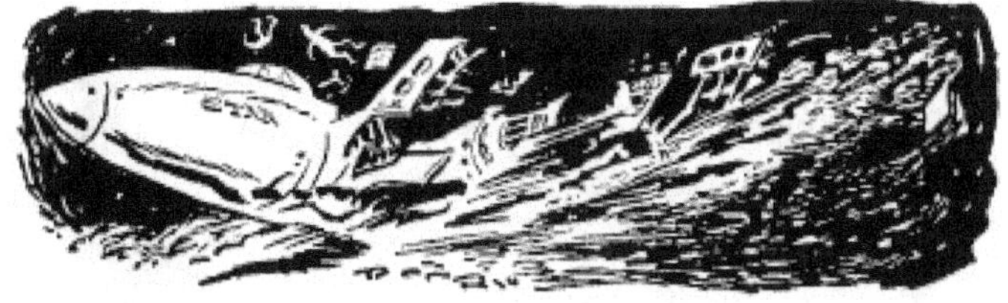

Evening Erotica with Gini Koch

Saturday 8.30pm-11.30pm - Xavier - Gini Koch and friends

Join Gini Koch, her Official Mod with the Most (Sass) Edward Pulley, the Blushing Meter, Joseph Gaxiola, and Gini's special guests: author Tom Leveen and the Two Gay Geeks podcast, as they teach you how to play the Euphemism Game! Guaranteed to be your most rollicking event at Westercon (and that's saying a lot). You're also guaranteed a little learning and a LOT of great prizes! (So many prizes! SO MANY!) For those who've attended before, you know you never know what to expect, including who might show up to "assist" with the game. For those who've only heard about what this event is like, now's your chance to experience it first hand! So come join Gini and get your euphemisms on! **Restricted to 18+.**

Found and Other Easy Electronics for Costumes and Props

Tuesday 10.30am-12.30pm - Capistrano - Jamie Hanrahan

This will be a fun show-and-tell panel where we'll see ways of lighting up your costume or prop with found, repurposed and inexpensive ready-to-use items - battery-operated Christmas tree lights, electroluminescent wire kits, etc. We will also answer questions (or at least point you to other resources) at all levels!

Happy 70th Anniversary, Roswell!

Sunday 3.30pm-4.30pm - Dolores - Gini Koch, Henry Vanderbilt, Connie Willis

Our panelists discuss their thoughts and observations on what they think really happened in Roswell 70 years ago. Was it a crashed UFO? Or a military surveillance balloon? How about a tourist trap conspiracy? Bring your own suggestions!

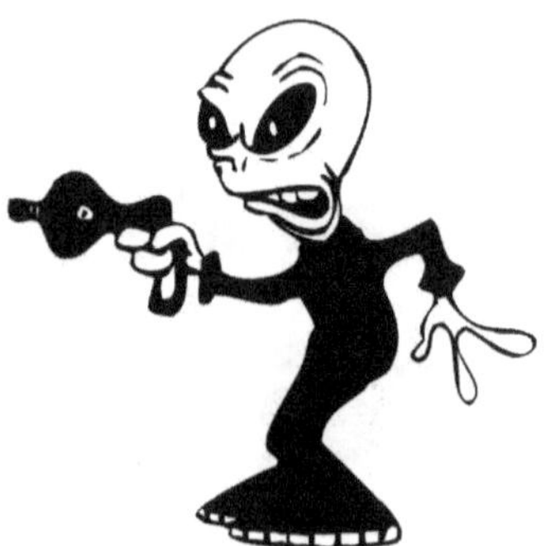

Hobbit Missed Connections

Saturday 2:00pm-3:00pm - Campanile - Khurt Khave, Katie Panveno, Alyssa Provan

An opinionated discussion of where the books and movies clashed, crashed and came together in all their Tolkien glory!

The Horror of Doctor Who

Saturday 3:30pm-4:30pm - Campanile - Crystel Flanders, Katie Panveno, Alyssa Provan, Chris Swanson

A look at the various villains throughout the show's long history that instil not just a sci-fi interest but a shudder and chills up the spine! Hold your companions close for this one, and remember, don't blink!

Horror Trivia Through The Ages

Sunday, 4.30pm-5.30pm - Campanile - Michael Flanders

Test your mettle in a battle of smarts with other participants to see who knows the most about modern and classical horror in various media!

How to Make Cordials and Zymurgy (Workshop)

Sunday, 2.00pm-whenever - Suite 3069 - Craig L. Dyer

The workshop will consist of making your own cordials, brewing info, mead and wine making. We will make two cordials - one "quickie" cordial ready for immediate consumption and one that will need time to set before consumption. Materials, other than alcohol, will be provided. You will need to bring a bottle of vodka (750 ml or greater). There will be some tasting of cordials.

Workshop is limited to 10 people 21+. You must provide a valid ID to participate or taste. Workshop fee is $15.

Kids' Alien Coloring Time

San Pedro, Sunday 9.00am-10.00am - TBD

Join us for a family friendly time coloring aliens. All supplies included. Prize for the best colored alien picture.

Kids' Costume Building

Saturday 12.30pm-1.30pm - San Pedro - Johnna Buttrick

Come and build a kid's costume. All supplies provided for free. The best costume will win a prize!

Match Game

Monday 8.00pm-11.00pm - Xavier - Kevin Standlee

Get ready to match the fannish stars! In this re-creation of the classic 1970s game show, contestants are selected randomly from the audience to attempt to match the panelists' answers to fill-in-the-blank questions like "Captain Kirk has the biggest ___ in Starfleet!"

All contestants will receive prizes.

Masquerade

Sunday, 8.00pm-10.00pm - Palm E/F - Diana Given

No sci-fi con is complete without a Masquerade! Ours is being organized by Elaine Mami, of the Lower Arizona Costume Enthusiasts, and MC'd by Diana Given, who co-runs the Arizona Steampunk Society and Wild Wild West Steampunk Convention.

Setup will be 4.30pm-6.30pm in Palm E/F, with rehearsal from 6.30pm-7.30pm. Masquerade Green Room is Dolores, open 6.30pm onwards.

The Mythology of Fillory and Further

Saturday 12:30pm-1:30pm - Campanile - Khurt Khave, Katie Panveno, Alyssa Provan

An in-depth discussion of the mythological connections between what mythos we've grown up with, and the mythos presented in the television show, *The Magician.*

Nerd Poetry Slam

Sunday 12.30pm-1.30pm - Cavetto - Jess Ballantyne, Tristan Marshell, Ernesto Moncada, Misako Yamazaki

The first ever Westercon Nerd Poetry Slam has arrived! Bring a poem, sign up on our state-of-the-art sign up sheet, and read your poem to those in attendance! Be judged by the Secret Council of Nerd Elders and you may win prizes! This is a free speech event, which means language could get coarse, subject matter could get troubling, and poets may get sexy. We welcome all poets, of all fandoms, of all races, creeds, planetary origins, orientations, of all genders or none! We want you! Props, costumes and musical accompaniment are welcomed! Try to keep your poems set within the time limit set by Poetry Slam Inc., 3-4 minutes. Sign up at the event.

Nerf Battle

Monday 9.30am-10.30am - San Pedro - The Royal Manticoran Navy

Join the Royal Manticoran Navy for a NERF battle in San Pedro! Bring your own NERF gun and leap into the fray!

The New Western Animation

Sunday 11.00am-12.00pm - Cavetto - Julie K. Verley

A discussion on how western animation has improved within the last twenty years (1990s to current). Look forward to a lively chat about your favorite animation programs from Cartoon Network, CN: Adult Swim to DisneyXD and Netflix, as well as the rise of independent animators and machinima artists on sites like YouTube.

Regency Dance

Saturday 7.00pm-9.00pm - Palm E/F - Alex Canto, John Hertz

Every Westercon has two dances, one of them a Regency Dance. Ours is presented by John Hertz and our Dance Co-ordinator, Alex Canto.

Shakespeare Goes Sci-Fi

Tuesday 12.30pm-1.30pm - Cavetto - Katherine Stewart

Join Shakespearean actress/director Katherine Stewart and test your ability to recognize famous sci-fi quotes, disguised as Shakespearean phrases! Warm up trading some of Shakespeare's insults with friends and then be quizzed on geeky lines from famous films! Can you find the original words wrapped up in Will's pretty lingo? Free for all ages! There will be prizes!

Sound Editing for Costumers

Sunday 9:30am-11:30am - Campanile - Jamie Hanrahan

Do you need to cut, edit, or extend a song for your presentation? Mix in narration and sound effects? This panel will introduce you to techniques you can use with freeware, shareware and professional sound-editing apps. We'll cover things like basic song cutting, extensions, mixing and cross-fading, voice-over recording and mixing, the all-important issue of level control and modification of sounds.

Three Toed Sock Hop

Monday 7.00pm-9.00pm - Palm E/F - Alex Canto

Our second dance is a Three Toed Sock Hop, on the theme that "Elvis is not dead; he just went home!"

Put on your dancing shoes and get down with some tunes that are out of this world! No matter if your flying saucer's blown its top, cut a rug with the cool cats! Costumes encouraged but not required: rockabilly Batman or pointy eared elvish impersonator; just grab an extra safety pin so you don't lose your cool, and it stays securely attached.

Trekker or Scruffy Nerf-Herder?

Monday 11.00am-12.00pm - Campanile - Michael Flanders

Star Wars vs. *Star Trek*: another trivia-based panel where the great struggle between franchises is continued. Do you think you know the Trek more than your friends? Can you list how many people held Luke Skywalker's lightsaber? Beam yourself up or make the jump to lightspeed and come have fun with fellow *Star Trek/Star Wars* trivia buffs!

Underlying Religious Tones in Star Wars

Saturday 5:00pm-6:00pm - Campanile - Khurt Khave, Katie Panveno, Alyssa Provan

A comparison of popular religion in our world vs. the *Star Wars* Universe, leaning heavily on the expanded universe across the books and coming together with the movies.

What Goes On Between Consenting Aliens?

Sunday 5.00pm-6.00pm - Xavier - Johnna Buttrick, H. Paul Honsinger, Gini Koch, T. L. Smith

Every wondered about how aliens have sex? We have. This panel will also have assorted alien sex toys on display for the panelists and audience to ponder and discuss their use.

What Makes a Compelling Villain?

Sunday 2.00pm-3.00pm - Cavetto - Joshua Cruz, Michael Flanders

From Darth Vader to Freddy Krueger and Loki to Kingpin, there are a plethora of villains that capture the attention of audiences both on film and television screens. But why do these characters grab our interest so heavily and why is it often more fun to root for the bad guy than the hero? This panel explores the characteristics and stories that offer the world a chance to talk about our fascination with the bad boys of books and films.

What's That Noise, Gang? We'd Better Go Check It Out

Sunday, 12.00pm-1.00pm - Campanile - Joshua Cruz, Jonathan Elliott, Crystel Flanders

A discussion about the reasons people like to be afraid and why we keep coming back to horror stories and films after being scared out of our wits!

Why We Just Can't Quit Game of Thrones *

Sunday 1.30pm-2.30pm - Campanile - Jacob Bailey, Jonathan Elliott, Crystel Flanders

Got *G.O.T.*? Westeros is a strange land of magic and murder. Many beloved characters have perished there to our cries of dismay or joy depending on the person. Here we will talk about our favorite characters, storylines, and religion as well as how the show follows/does not follow the books. We will also be speculating on future plot points which will include a mini game of "name the next to die".

*Warning! Spoilers, darling!

Young Pirate Training

Saturday 5.00pm-6.00pm - San Pedro - The DREAD Fleet

Come join the Pirates of the DREAD Fleet as we train "cabin monkeys" in the ways of piracy!All are welcome, as long as you're a kid! Meet the greatest ne'er-do-wells that ever were. Fight, sing and live like a pirate!

Your Ringwraith is No Match for My White Walker

Sunday 9:30am-10:30am - Ironstone - Michael Flanders

It's Tolkien vs. Martin: a trivia-based panel in which participants must identify facts about J. R. R. Tolkien or George R. R. Martin and the various media that represent their work.

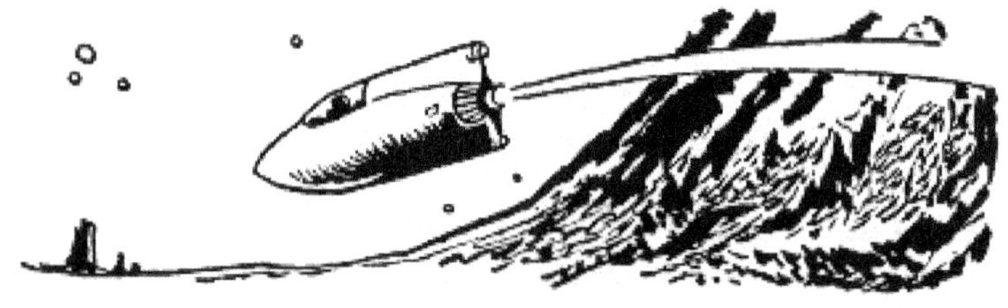

Science

911 in Space! Handling Medical Emergencies in Freefall

Tuesday, 9.00am-10.00am - Augustine - Bruce Davis

Injury and illness don't look the same in microgravity and dealing with it when you can't send someone to the hospital can be challenging. NASA has some interesting solutions and some scary decisions about what can and can't be done.

And the Winner Is... Privatization of Space

Monday 3.00pm-4.00pm - Augustine - Stephen Fleming, Alfred Nash, Henry Vanderbilt

What are the benefits and drawbacks of the privatization of space? Join Alfred Nash, Stephen Fleming and our Science GoH, Henry Vanderbilt, for an in depth look at the pros and cons.

Boldly Going for Fifty Years: *Star Trek*'s Impacts on Science, Technology and Society

Monday 4.30pm-5.30pm - Augustine - Bjo & John Trimble, Dr. Dave Williams

In September 1966, the first episode of *Star Trek* aired on NBC. NASA was still three years short of landing people on the Moon, yet the innovative series was soon zipping viewers light years beyond the Solar System every week. How has it impacted our world? Join the Trimbles and Dave Williams to explore the topic.

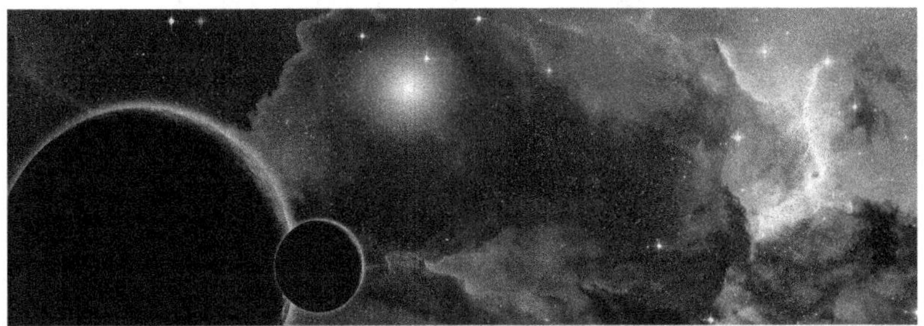

Breakfast with the Scientists: Cryonics Update Today

Sunday 7.30am-whenever - Mission Grille - Bruce Davis, Steve Howe

Join Bruce Davis over breakfast to hear about what's happening in cryonics and suspended animation. Hosted by Steve Howe.

Breakfast with the Scientists: Getting There from Here, Affordably

Tuesday 7.30am-whenever - Mission Grille - Steve Howe, Henry Vanderbilt

Join Science Guest of Honor Henry Vanderbilt over breakfast to see how we can make it from down here all the way up there without breaking the bank. Hosted by Steve Howe.

Breakfast with the Scientists: To the Moon and Mars or Bust

Monday 7.30am-whenever - Mission Grille - Stephen Fleming, Steve Howe

Join Stephen Fleming over breakfast to discuss the ins and outs of a return to the Moon and whether we are ready for a manned trip to Mars yet. Hosted by Steve Howe.

Exoplanets: Discovering Planets Outside the Solar System

Monday 9.00am-10.00am - Augustine - David Lee Summers

Join astronomer and author David Lee Summers on a trip outside the solar system for an exploration of exoplanets.

Exploring the Red Planet: What Could We Be Doing?

Monday 9.30am-10.30am - Dolores - Steve Howe

Mars is a hostile place - little atmosphere, cold, and very dry - maybe. Survival on Mars will require using the local resources, novel technologies for power and propulsion that would enable rapid exploration of Mars. What could we be doing that we aren't?

Eye in the Martian Sky: Mars Reconnaissance Orbiter

Tuesday 11.00am-12.00pm - Dolores - Bridget Landry

MRO not only observes Mars, but it also supports landed missions by scouting landing sites and relaying their data once they arrive. Come hear a former member of MRO's operations team speak about how we study Mars and the vast amount we have learned.

How Do We Get to the Stars? A Propulsion Roadmap

Tuesday 12.30pm-1.30pm - Jokake - Steve Howe

Current propulsion barely gets us to the Moon. Much more advanced concepts must be developed to go to Mars and beyond. Steve Howe will cover near term nuclear rockets up through antimatter.

Intelligent Tool-Using Dinosaurs: Would We Know?

Tuesday 3.30pm-4.30pm - Dolores - Steve Howe

Dinosaurs lived on the Earth for 250 million years; Homo Sapiens only 0.3 million. Were there entire civilizations of which we know nothing? This is the basis of Steve Howe's novel *Wrench and Claw.*

It Doesn't Work that Way: Accurate Science in Science Fiction

Sunday 4.30pm-5.30pm - Augustine - David Lee Summers, Daina Wright

Why is accurate science in science fiction important? Join Daina Wright and David Lee Summers to find out.

Last Year Today in Space

Sunday 3.00pm-4.00pm - Augustine - Dan Dubrick, Stephen Fleming

What advances are being made in space exploration and travel?

Meet Henry Vanderbilt

Saturday 1.30pm-2.30pm - Augustine - Henry Vanderbilt

Henry Vanderbilt founded the Space Access Society in 1992, and ran the quietly influential annual Space Access Conferences in most of the years since. He is not a rocket scientist, but he can translate reasonably well between rocket scientist and English. (He did manage a bunch of rocket engineers once, but that's another story.)

He first started working for radically cheaper space transportation via fast-turnaround fuel-and-go reusable rockets back in 1986, when that was all strictly SF. He's a lifelong Fan but he's nevertheless pleased as hell to see this plot device now doing a genre jump to current-day technothriller. He looks forward to it soon settling down as just another taken-for-granted background element in mainstream contemporary literature.

Picking up the Spare: New Horizons at Pluto

Tuesday 9.30am-10.30am - Dolores - Bridget Landry

Pluto, last of the (former) planets to be explored, saved a few surprises for us. Come see the pictures and hear the latest theories about this remarkable object.

Psyche: Journey to a Metal World

Monday 10.30am-11.30am - Augustine - Dr. Dave Williams

For the first time Arizona State University will be at the forefront of the development and operations of a NASA planetary mission! On January 4, 2017 ASU was selected to develop the Psyche Discovery mission, the first spacecraft to visit a world made of metal, asteroid 16 Psyche. Join Dr. David Williams of ASU's School of Earth & Space Exploration, and a member of the Psyche Science Team, to learn about this exciting new mission of discovery.

Rescuing the Future: We Went to the Moon! Then Stalled

Part 1: Sunday 12.00pm-1.00pm - Augustine - Henry Vanderbilt

Part 2: Sunday 1.30pm-2.30pm - Augustine - Henry Vanderbilt

In the fifties, science fiction's vision of how we might expand off this planet went mainstream in *Colliers Magazine*. In the sixties we went to the Moon! But then for decades our bright future in space stalled. An insider's look at what went wrong and how this vision of the future was then reinvented, sold all over again from the 1980s onward and is now finally beginning to happen.

Ringworld Revealed: Discoveries from NASA's Cassini Mission to Saturn

Sunday 9.00am-10.00am - Augustine - Bridget Landry, Dr. Dave Williams

Dr. Dave Williams first presented at Westercon 57 just after NASA's Cassini Mission arrived at Saturn July 4 weekend 2004. Thirteen years later, what has been learned? Join Dr. Dave of ASU's School of Earth & Space Exploration and Bridget Landry for a review of results from Cassini and what has been discovered about Saturn and its rings and moons.

Science/Education Track Overview

Saturday 12.00pm-1.00pm - Augustine - KellyAnn Bonnell

Join Science/Education track coordinator KellyAnn Bonnell for an overview of the programming for Science and Education at this year's Westercon, including the Unconference to be held on Tuesday, July 4.

Tabby's Star: Are Aliens Trying to Communicate?

Monday 12.00pm-1.00pm - Augustine - Keith Henson

Are aliens trying to communicate with us? Join Keith Henson to learn about the highly unusual KIC 8462852, better known as Tabby's Star, after Tabetha S. Boyajian, lead author of its initial study.

Team X Activate!

Sunday 10.30am-11.30am - Augustine - Alfred Nash

The JPL Advanced Projects Design Team, also known as Team X, is an interdisciplinary team of engineers that utilizes "concurrent engineering methodologies" to complete rapid design, analysis and evaluation of mission concept designs. Join Team X lead engineer Alfred Nash for insight into the work they do.

Time Travel Via Cryonics

Monday 3.30pm-4.30pm - Dolores - Keith Henson

Time travel is always a chancy business. Cryonics as a way to travel into the future comes with no guarantees, but it's the only way we know of now that might work (other than just living that is). So if you would like to hear from people who have been signed up for decades and ask them questions, come to this talk.

Unpanels

Tuesday, 10.30am-11.00am, 12.00am-1.00pm, 1.30pm-2.30pm - Augustine

Unpanels are panels that are created *at the con*. Attendees choose the topics and the presenters. Voting will happen through the course of the weekend and the Unpanels will be held on Tuesday, July 4.

Year of the Dwarf Planet

Saturday 3.00pm-4.00pm - Augustine - Dr. Dave Williams

Results from NASA's Dawn Mission to Ceres and New Horizons Mission to Pluto. NASA completed the initial reconnaissance of our Solar System with the New Horizons spacecraft flyby of Pluto in July 2015 and the Dawn orbiter of Ceres beginning in March 2015. Join Dr. Dave Williams of ASU's School of Earth & Space Exploration, and a member of the Dawn Science Team, to review the major results of these latest missions of discovery!

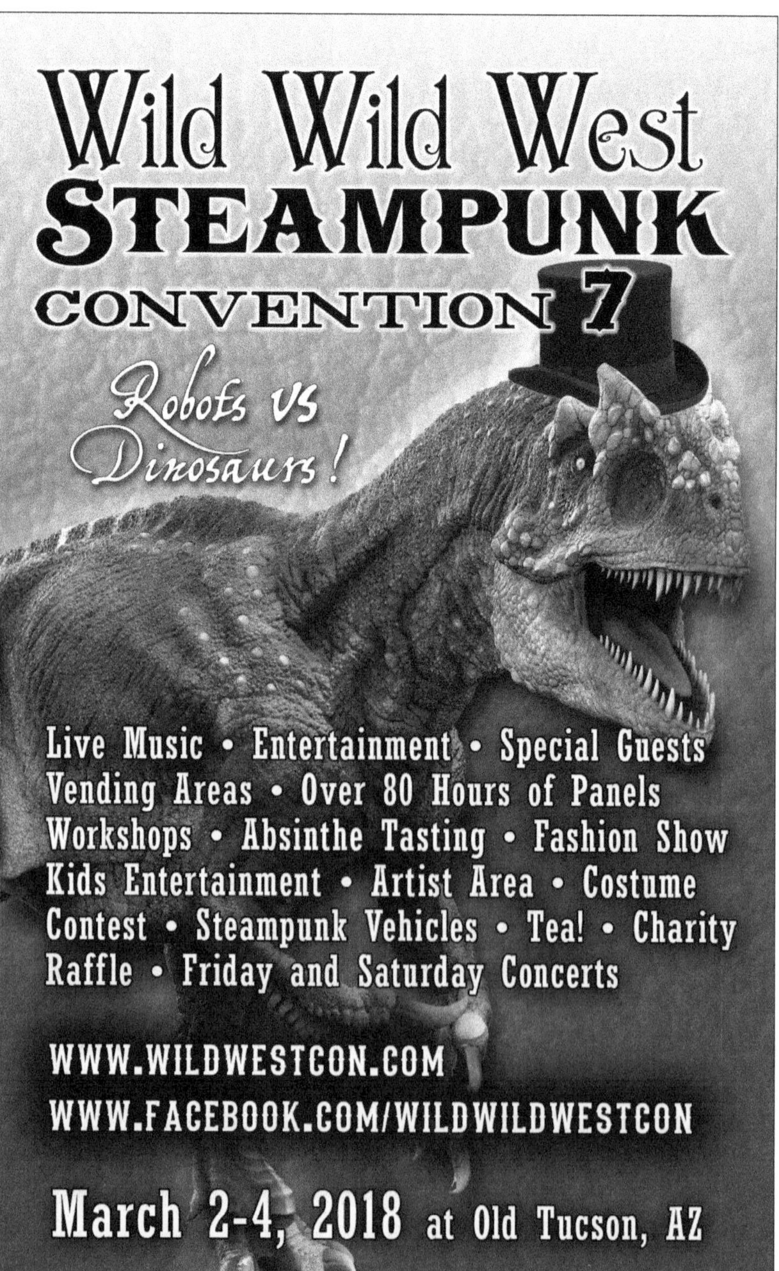
Wild Wild West
STEAMPUNK
CONVENTION 7
Robots vs Dinosaurs!
Live Music • Entertainment • Special Guests
Vending Areas • Over 80 Hours of Panels
Workshops • Absinthe Tasting • Fashion Show
Kids Entertainment • Artist Area • Costume
Contest • Steampunk Vehicles • Tea! • Charity
Raffle • Friday and Saturday Concerts
WWW.WILDWESTCON.COM
WWW.FACEBOOK.COM/WILDWILDWESTCON
March 2-4, 2018 at Old Tucson, AZ

Steampunk

Arizona Penny Dreadfuls Guide to Victorian Weirdness

Monday 2.00pm-3.00pm - Xavier - Khurt Khave, Asp Zelazny

Join those delightful reprobates, the Arizona Penny Dreadfuls, for a discussion on just how weird those Victorians got.

Bartitsu Demonstration

Sunday 11.00am-12.00pm - Palm E/F - Dirk Folmer

Bartitsu, the lost martial art of Sherlock Holmes... almost! Bartitsu, the first Mixed Martial Art, was developed in 1899 and became a huge success in England. Many articles appear in period magazines, like *Pearson's*, but, for multiple reasons, virtually disappeared by 1904. The panel will delve into the history, theory and mechanics of this fascinating martial art.

Coloring Fun for Steampunks

Tuesday 9.30am-10.30am - San Pedro - Countess Chaos

Come color with us! These days, coloring has become a cool and relaxing activity for everyone. Color pages, crayons, markers and colored pencils will be supplied. Steampunk, Victorian and Cthulhu color pages.

Cosplay Like a Pro! Prop and Armor Building

Saturday 2.00pm-3.00pm - Sand Lotus - Allen Amis, Anabel Amis, Frank and Nat's Armory, Justin Hackert, KnowOne's Designs

Award-winning cosplayers give you the run-down on translating screenshots and concept art into actual costumes through a plethora of accessible armor, prop and costume-building techniques. This panel includes an open Q&A, so bring your questions and cosplay like a pro!

A Courtesy of Compliments: Compliment Duelling

Sunday 3.30pm-4.30pm - Xavier - Madame Askew, Katherine Stewart

Whether it's compliments at 50 paces, courtesies at dawn or gallantry until first blush, Compliment Duelling has settled matters of honour, averted terrible strife and resulted in a few famous engagements. Join our hosts as they teach this honourable and ancient art and host a tourney.

Diving into Corsets: Maker Tips, Urban Myths and Legendary Looks

Monday 12.30pm-1.30pm - Palm E/F - Madame Askew

Join Madame Askew as she divulges her wisdom, anecdotes and tips on corsetry. From making your own to buying a ready-made corset, Madame Askew will share her knowledge and debunk the myths as she discusses just how to get a great corseted look!

Do the Bustle

Sunday 12.30pm-1.30pm - Xavier - Madame Askew, Katherine Stewart

Learn more about the bustle, how and why they came into being. Our panel will discuss from the basic dainty bump to the full elaborate cage, and what goes into making one.

Fan Workshop

Sunday 5.00pm-6.00pm - San Pedro - Johnna Buttrick

Come make and decorate your own paper fan. Water colors and fan provided. **$5 per fan.**

The Future of Steampunk in Writing

Sunday 11.00am-12.00pm - Jokake - Arlys Holloway, David Lee Summers, Vaughn Treude

Where do you see the future of steampunk writing going? Join our panel of steampunk authors to find out what they think.

How to Write a Steampunk Sonnet: You Can Be a Steam Poet

Tuesday 2.00pm-3.00pm - Campanile - Katherine Stewart

You too can wax poetic with your steamy comrades! Learn the design and structure of a sonnet, and then have the skills to make your own. But poetry is hard, you say! Nah, it's really not. Work with Shakespearean actor/writer, Katherine Stewart to create your own steampunk sonnet masterpiece. We'll cover: What is a sonnet? How are they put together? We're putting steampunk elements in there? Really? Can I write one of my own? A panel for writers, readers, aficionados, and dilettantes. By the end of the panel, you will have a completed sonnet to lord over your friends!

H. P. Lovecraft and the Cthulhu Mythos

Monday 7.00pm-8.00pm - Dolores - Khurt Khave

Local cultists, the First United Church of Cthulhu, discuss the work of prophet and horror author H. P. Lovecraft, the Cthulhu Mythos, and everything tentacles. Trivia and prizes! **Restricted to 18+.**

Mask Decorating 101

Monday 11.00am-12.00pm - San Pedro - TBD

Join us for tips and ideas on how to take a basic mask and make it special. We'll have markers, crayons, feathers and other assorted goodies on hand to decorate with. All supplies are free.

Memento Mori: Death in the Victorian Era

Friday 9.00pm-10.00pm - Dolores - Khurt Khave

The traditions, practices, and superstitions of death during the 19th century. Slideshow included. Not for the faint of heart! Images of actual dead bodies and beyond. **Restricted to 18+.**

Molding and Casting for Beginning and Advanced Costumers

Sunday 5.00pm-6.00pm - Jokake - Allen Amis, Anabel Amis, KnowOne's Designs, Thermo Cosplay

New to the world of molding and casting? Award-winning cosplayers will show you how to reproduce prop items made from a variety of materials - leather, clay, wood and more! We will also cover the challenges that occur from molding and casting (and what to do when everything seems to be going wrong). This panel includes an open Q&A.

Moustache Wax Workshop

Sunday 3.30pm-4.30pm - San Pedro - Dirk Folmer

Professor Theodoric Brandywine, the Man, the Myth, the Moustache! The Professor will teach you how you can cheaply and *easily* make your own moustache wax, beard balm, and beard oil, from high quality all natural ingredients, that is *better* than many commercially available products at a fraction of their cost. This is a Make and Take, all supplies included. **$15 per person** or free if you only want the information.

Parasol Painting Workshop (Freestyle)

Sunday 10.30am-12.30pm - San Pedro - Rebecca Carter, Tracey Feltes

This class usually takes 2 hours, depending on the complexity of your design. Provided items are a 32-inch paper parasol, paint, brushes, glitter, stencils, sponges and rubber gloves. To get the most out of your class time, think of your design ahead of time. Feel free to bring your own stencils. You are encouraged to wear clothing that you don't mind getting a little paint spilled on. **$20 per person.**

Parasol Painting Workshop (Kaylee)

San Pedro, Sunday 1.00pm-3.00pm - San Pedro - Rebecca Carter, Tracey Feltes

As above for all details and caveats, but for this class, your parasol will come with a very light charcoal pre-outline stripe to help get you started. **$20 per person.**

Picture Frame Workshop

Tuesday 2.00pm-3.00pm - San Pedro - Countess Chaos

Paint and decorate your own personal steampunk frame. Assorted wooden frames to choose from. Paint, rub 'n buff, gears and decorative accessories included. **Cost is $10 per frame.**

Rub 'n Buff Gun Workshop

Saturday 2.00pm-3.00pm - San Pedro - Countess Chaos

Personalize your own gun to fit your style. Gun, rub 'n buff, gears and accessories will be provided. Free to attend but those taking part must buy a gun: **Small $2, Medium $5, Nerf Maverick $25**.

Sex in the Victorian Era

Saturday 7.00pm-8.00pm - Xavier - Khurt Khave

They weren't as uptight as you think. Learn about brothels, burlesque, the world's first adult toys, the beginning of the pornography industry, plus much more. Slideshow included. **Restricted to 18+.**

Splendid Teapot Racing: ConAlope Convivial

Tuesday 11.00am-12.00pm - Palm E/F - Madame Askew

A beloved steampunk sport, Splendid Teapot Racing launched itself from the far distant shores of New Zealand to land via mad science in the deserts of Arizona. Join in the race yourself or cheer on adventurous makers from across the West as they navigate blood curdling challenges like the Ramp of Doom, the Chasm of Death, and the Teeter Totter of Terror. Sign up in advance to ensure your spot in the tourney!

Steampunk Before It Was Steampunk

Monday 5.00pm-6.00pm - Cavetto - Arlys Holloway, Vaughn Treude

K. W. Jeter coined the term "steampunk" in a letter to *Locus* in 1987, but the genre existed before then without a name. This panel is a discussion of films, TV shows and books that were steampunk before it was steampunk.

Steampunk Roundtable

Monday 3.30pm-4.30pm - Jokake - Madame Askew, Dirk Folmer, Katherine Stewart, David Lee Summers

What makes steampunk an enduring pop culture phenomenon? Attend this roundtable discussion of steampunk with contributors in varied fields.

Stylish Steamy Hair Clip Workshop

Tuesday 11.00am-12.00pm - San Pedro - Countess Chaos

In this workshop we will create lovely steamy hair clips to add to your steampunk collection. Filigree, clip, gears and other ornaments included. **Cost is $8.00 per clip**.

Tea Duelling Grudge Match: Weasel vs. Askew!

Sunday 2.30pm-3.30pm - Suite 4017 - Khurt Khave, Madame Askew

In the storied traditions of Tea Duelling, there are many legendary rivalries and tea duelling battles. The grudge between the Dirty Weasel and Madame Askew stands as a testament to the razor honed wit and keenly balanced bickies that betoken a master tea duellist. Come for the tea duelling, stay for the repartee!

Teapot Racing 101

Monday 9.30pm-10.30pm - Jokake - Asp Zelazny

The who, what, where, when and whether there's a why of the amazing sport of Splendid Teapot Racing.

Tesla vs. Edison: Electrifying Trivia

Monday 12.30pm-1.30pm - Campanile - Michael Flanders

Come test your knowledge with this trivia game of quotes and facts about these famous inventors.

Tipsy Tea Duelling

date/time TBD - ConSuite

Tipsy tea duelling will occur in the ConSuite at a date/time still to be determined. It may even break out at random moments just because. Be warned, though: tea duelling is a dangerous sport conducted sober, but it reaches the levels of legend when conducted tipsy.

Tipsy tea duelling in the ConSuite is sponsored in memory of Arizona fan, costume designer and lover of color, Lars Morgan.

Trinket Box Workshop

Tuesday 2.00pm-3.00pm - San Pedro - Countess Chaos

Paint and decorate your own personal steampunk trinket box. Assorted wooden boxes to choose from. Paint, gears, and accessories included. Feel free to bring any special items you would like to add. **Cost is $8 per box.**

Unarmed Tactic Demonstration

Monday 11.00am-12.00pm - Palm E/F - Dirk Folmer

Bartitsu, Le Canne, Savate and English bare knuckle boxing... Professor Theodoric Brandywine has studied them all and he will be giving a live demonstration of how a Proper Gentleman would defend himself and his companions from Ruffians. There will also be an interactive seminar on the basics of Le Canne, so bring your Walking Stick. Self defense is not only for Gentlemen! Ladies, the Professor will also introduce self defense with a parasol, and give a brief talk about the Ju Jitsu Suffragettes!

Victorian Flirting: The Language of the Fan

Saturday 12.30pm-1.30pm - Sand Lotus - Katherine Stewart

Calling all dandies and darlings! Steampunk ladies (and cosmopolitan gentlemen) learn how to flirt elegantly without saying a word. The fan is a stylish and versatile accessory that can communicate volumes. Join Bustle Girl (Katherine Stewart) to discover the wonderful, coquettish secrets that unfold in the pleats of a fan! Open to both male and female, the romantic code of fan language unlocks a world of flirtation and communication.

Whose Crumpet is It Anyway?

Monday 5.00pm-6.00pm - Palm E/F - Madame Askew

Once the costume is in place and the character created, use improv to breath life into your persona and add verve to photographs. Madame Askew will discuss some of her tricks for improv and invite attendees to join in a few interactive games.

You Made That Costume Out of WHAT?!

Saturday 3.30pm-4.30pm - Sand Lotus - Anabel Amis, Allen Amis, Justin Hackert

You can repurpose almost anything for costuming. Watch a panel of designers show you how to make incredible costumes and props out of everyday items to fit into wasteland, steampunk, sci-fi, fantasy and more! This panel includes an open Q&A.

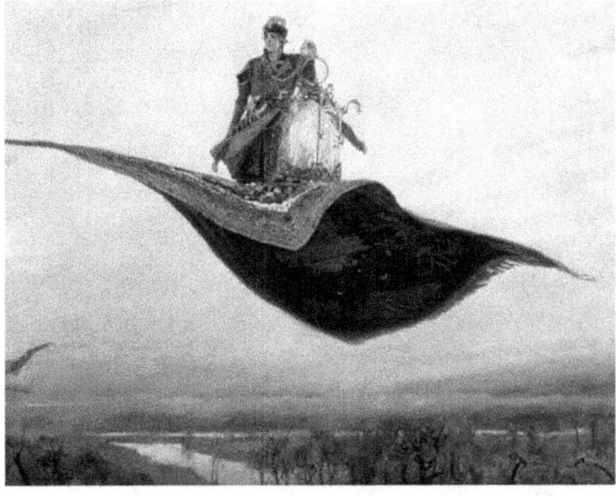

Membership List

Membership (Listed by Number) | (g)= 'guest of' (s) = supporting

W0001 Dee Astell
W0002 Hal C. F. Astell
W0003 Julie Dillon
W0004 Tom Deadstuff
W0005 Larry Elmore
W0006 Connie Willis
W0007 Gini Koch
W0008 Henry Vanderbilt
W0009 Tim Griffin
W0010 Bjo Trimble
W0011 John Trimble
W0012 Ron Ontell
W0013 Kevin McAlonan
W0014 Val Ontell
W0015 Weston Ochse
W0016 Brian Abernathy
W0017 Linda Addison
W0018 Jerrie M. Adkins
W0019 Jonnene Alders
W0020 Mark Ayala
W0021 Allen Amis
W0022 Anabel Amis
W0023 Gary Andrews
W0024 SL Art
W0025 Bruce Arthurs
W0026 John Autore
W0027 Garrick Backer
W0028 Jackie Backer
W0029 Jacob Bailey
W0030 Kim Bailey
W0031 Jess Ballantyne
W0032 Mari Bangs
W0033 Mari Bangs (g)
W0034 Stephanie L. Bannon
W0035 Roxanne Barlow
W0036 Roxanne Barlow (child of)
W0037 Kathryn M. Baron
W0038 Kathryn M. Baron (g)
W0039 Debbie Bayliss
W0040 Debbie Bayliss (g)
W0041 Kuma Bear
W0042 Bob Beckwith
W0043 Bob Beckwith (g)
W0044 Bernard Bell
W0045 Bernard Bell
W0046 Judith Bemis
W0047 Jan Bender
W0048 Jan Bender (g)
W0049 Del Benjamin
W0050 Cynthia Berens
W0051 James Berens
W0052 Len Berger
W0053 John Bernardi
W0054 Penni Beveridge
W0055 Nathan Blackwell
W0056 John Blake
W0057 John Blake (g)
W0058 Tia Bly

W0059 Maya Bohnhoff
W0060 R. Merrill Bollerud
W0061 Mark Boniece
W0062 Jon Bonnell
W0063 KellyAnn Bonnell
W0064 Catherine Book
W0065 Tiffany Branum
W0066 Seth Breidbart
W0067 Alexandra Brown
W0068 Grant Brown
W0069 Jordan Brown
W0070 Kim Brown
W0071 Troy Brown
W0072 Warren Buff
W0073 Victor Bugg
W0074 Manny Burruel
W0075 Johnna Buttrick
W0076 Jo Ann Byrne
W0077 Chuck Cady
W0078 Katrine Cady
W0079 Tasha Cady
W0080 Alex Canto
W0081 Ashley Carlson
W0082 Claudia Caro
W0083 Mateo Caro
W0084 Noe Caro
W0085 Amy Carpenter
W0086 Amy Carpenter (g)
W0087 Jason Youngdale (g)
W0088 Mark Catalfano
W0089 Catherine Chambers
W0090 Peri Charlifu (s)
W0091 Nikki Chase
W0092 Craig Chenery
W0093 Walter Chisholm
W0094 Richard Christ
W0095 David Clark
W0096 David Clark (g)
W0097 Keda Clark
W0098 Sarah Clemens
W0099 Shelbie Cline
W0100 Steve Coltrin
W0101 Joseph Cook
W0102 Paul Cook
W0103 Steven Cook
W0104 Daniel Cortopassi
W0105 Jeannie Cox
W0106 Thomas Cox
W0107 Richard Crawford
W0108 Richard Crawford (g)
W0109 Joshua Cruz
W0110 Craig Curtis
W0111 Jennifer Czepiel (Jenn Czep)
W0112 Michael D'Ambrosio
W0113 Ryan Dalton
W0114 Joni Brill Dashoff (s)
W0115 Todd Dashoff (s)
W0116 Avery Davis
W0117 Bruce Davis
W0118 Debbie Gorden Davis
W0119 (withheld)
W0120 Clark Denning
W0121 Jane Dennis (s)
W0122 Scott Dennis (s)
W0123 Emily Devenport
W0124 Laura Domitz (s)

W0125 James Doty (J. L. Doty)
W0126 Richard Draude
W0127 Jason Drotman
W0128 Michael F. Duckett Jr.
W0129 Michael F. Duckett Sr.
W0130 Donna Dudley
W0131 Braden Duncan (s)
W0132 Brian Duncan (s)
W0133 Kevin DumCum
W0134 Craig L. Dyer
W0135 Nikki Ebright
W0136 Thomas Eivins
W0137 Jacqueline T. Elderkin
W0138 Eva M Eldridge
W0139 Jonathan Elliott
W0140 Brian Esterson
W0141 Charlene Estrada
W0142 Mark Ewbank
W0143 Michael Falinski
W0144 Bruce Farr (s)
W0145 Marcus Fields
W0146 Erika Finbraaten
W0147 Jason Youngdale
W0148 Leslie Fish
W0149 Leslie Fish (g)
W0150 Charles Fisher
W0151 Charles Fisher (g)
W0152 Crystel Flanders
W0153 Michael Flanders
W0154 Shawn Flanders
W0155 Stephen Fleming
W0156 Dirk Folmer
W0157 Jesse D. Foster
W0158 Susan Fox
W0159 Janie Franz
W0160 Laura Freas
W0161 Laura Freas (g)
W0162 Alisa Frisch
W0163 Benjamin Frisch
W0164 Stephany Gallegos
W0165 Charles Galway (s)
W0166 Joseph Gaxiola
W0167 Corey Gehman
W0168 Jeff George
W0169 Gilead
W0170 Kerrie Gimmler
W0171 David Gish
W0172 Glenn Glazer (s)
W0173 Jerry Gobler
W0174 Jean Goddin
W0175 Barry Gold
W0176 Lee Gold
W0177 Lynn Gold
W0178 Patrick L. Gomez
W0179 Michael Goodwin (s)
W0180 Michael Goodwin (g) (s)
W0181 Michael Goodwin (g) (s)
W0182 Michael Goodwin (g) (s)
W0183 Margaret Grady
W0184 William Green
W0185 Mark Greenawalt
W0186 Sandra Greenberg
W0187 Vaughan Grey
W0188 Katie Griffith
W0189 Brian Gross
W0190 Peter Gryffin

W0191 Peter Gryffin (g)
W0192 Justin Hackert
W0193 Paul Haidinger
W0194 Francis Hamit
W0195 Francis Hamit (g)
W0196 Jamie Hanrahan
W0197 Harold Harrigan (s)
W0198 Harold Harrigan III (s)
W0199 Lisa Deutsch Harrigan (s)
W0200 Donald F. Harrington
W0201 Donald F. Harrington (g)
W0202 Ben Hatcher
W0203 Kate Hatcher
W0204 Eric Haury
W0205 Lisa Hayes
W0206 Earl C. Hedges Jr.
W0207 Keith Henson
W0208 Felicia Herman
W0209 Allison Hershey (s)
W0210 John Hertz
W0211 Kevin Hewett (g)
W0212 Kevin Hewett
W0213 M. R. Hildebrand
W0214 Jeffrey Hintz
W0215 Jeffrey Hintz (g)
W0216 Jose Ho-Guanipa
W0217 Ernest Hogan
W0218 Paul Honsinger
W0219 Conrad Horning
W0220 Honor Horning
W0221 Mark E. Horning
W0222 Jennifer Horning
W0223 Sage Horning
W0224 Steve Howe
W0225 Kevin Hull
W0226 Patti Hultstrand
W0227 Patti Hultstrand (g)
W0228 (withheld)
W0229 (withheld)
W0230 Jonathan Jackson
W0231 Brenda Jameson
W0232 Brenda Jameson (g)
W0233 Curtis Jefferson
W0234 Dawn Jeffory-Nelson
W0235 Brad Jensen
W0236 Lyn Jeppsen (s)
W0237 Ryan Johannes
W0238 Ryan Johannes
W0239 Deena Jo Johnson
W0240 Marcus Johnston
W0241 Lamont Jones
W0242 Mitzi Jones
W0243 Meredith Julian
W0244 Andrew Kallen
W0245 Melissa Katano
W0246 Sakura (Chelsea) Kelsey
W0247 Paul Kennedy
W0248 Khurt Khave
W0249 Judith Kindell (s)
W0250 Jennifer Kinghorn
W0251 Eric T. Knight
W0252 Eric T. Knight (g)
W0253 Bill Knight (s)
W0254 Diana Koivunen
W0255 Erick Kostiw
W0256 Rick Kovalcik

W0257 Peter Kral
W0258 Debra Krol
W0259 Gordon Kuist
W0260 Tabitha Ladin (s)
W0261 Bridget Landry
W0262 Bridget Landry (g)
W0263 David Larsen
W0264 Suzanne Lazear
W0265 Mary E. Lee (s)
W0266 Michael Lesnick
W0267 Tom Leveen
W0268 Erin Lewis
W0269 Jeffrey L. Lewis
W0270 Jacqueline Lichtenberg
W0271 Jacqueline Lichtenberg (g)
W0272 Syd Logsdon
W0273 Arel Lucas
W0274 Bradford Lyau
W0275 Gloria Magid
W0276 Gloria Magid (g) (s)
W0277 Elaine Mami
W0278 Katrina Manis
W0279 Jim Manning
W0280 Sandra Manning
W0281 Beth Marble
W0282 Chris Marble
W0283 Griffin Maria
W0284 Jeff Mariotte
W0285 Tristan Marshell
W0286 Susan Martin
W0287 Alice Massoglia
W0288 Marty Massoglia
W0289 Theresa Mather (s)
W0290 Tracey Maye
W0291 Richard McAllister
W0292 Richard McAllister (g)
W0293 Jen McAlonan
W0294 Shelby McBride
W0295 Keith McClune
W0296 Sheila McClune
W0297 John McDougal
W0298 Cathy McManamon
W0299 Althea McMurrian
W0300 George A. McUrso (s)
W0301 Cary Meriwether
W0302 Gwen Merriman
W0303 Stellar Millar
W0304 Moebius Enterprises
W0305 Moebius Enterprises
W0306 Deirdre Saoirse Moen (s)
W0307 Rick Moen (s)
W0308 June Moffatt (s)
W0309 Jaziel Beltran Molina
W0310 Ernesto Moncada
W0311 Jesus Sebastian Mora
W0312 Cathy Mullican
W0313 Jonathan Muraca
W0314 Marguerite T. Murray
W0315 Eric Nabity
W0316 Katherine Nabity
W0317 Alfred Nash
W0318 Alfred Nash (g)
W0319 Alfred Nash (g)
W0320 Yvonne Navarro
W0321 Catherine Neff
W0322 Brigid Nelson (s)

W0323 Bob Nelson
W0324 Shaun Nelson
W0325 Amy Nichols
W0326 Larry Niven (s)
W0327 Samantha Nocera
W0328 Susan Nock
W0329 Susan Nock (g)
W0330 Rick Novy
W0331 Ronald Oakes
W0332 Tara Oakes
W0333 George R. O'Barts Jr.
W0334 George R. O'Barts Jr. (g)
W0335 Norman T. O'Dell
W0336 Christina O'Halloran (s)
W0337 John O'Halloran (s)
W0338 Sean Oliver
W0339 Brian Olnick
W0340 Richard Olson
W0341 Ian O'Neil
W0342 (withheld)
W0343 Richard O'Shea (s)
W0344 John Owen
W0345 Tony Padegimas
W0346 Chris Paige (s)
W0347 Jean Palmer (s)
W0348 David Lee Pancake (s)
W0349 Katie Panveno
W0350 Anna Paradox
W0351 Amanda Parker
W0352 Tony Parker
W0353 Elayne Pelz
W0354 Thomas Perry
W0355 Clare Peters-Libeu
W0356 Sharon Pierce (s)
W0357 Michelle Pincus
W0358 Eylat Poliner
W0359 Mark Poliner (s)
W0360 Alyssa Provan
W0361 Edward Pulley
W0362 Nora Rankin
W0363 Jamie Wyman Reddy
W0364 Daniel Reyes
W0365 Regina Reynante (s)
W0366 Noah Richman
W0367 Kat Rider
W0368 Valerie Ritchie
W0369 Andrea Rittschof
W0370 Duncan Rittschof
W0371 Frankie Robertson
W0372 Linda Louise Robinett
W0373 Dawndreia Robinson
W0374 Janet G. Robinson
W0375 Kevin Roche (s)
W0376 Marsheila Rockwell
W0377 (withheld)
W0378 Rebecca Rowan
W0379 Ralph J. Ryan (s)
W0380 David Rybacki
W0381 Walter Sanville
W0382 Patrick Sattler
W0383 Bruce W. Saul
W0384 Sharon Sbarsky
W0385 Isabel Schechter (s)
W0386 Paul Schmidt
W0387 Gene Schneider (s)
W0388 Kathi Schreiber

W0389 Chris Schretzman
W0390 Michael Senft
W0391 Annette Sexton-Ruiz
W0392 Raye Seyberth
W0393 Raye Seyberth (g)
W0394 Jim Shibley
W0395 Charles Shimada
W0396 Michael F. Siladi
W0397 Jocelynne Simone
W0398 Sharon Skinner
W0399 Stacy Smith
W0400 Terry Smith
W0401 Terry Smith (g)
W0402 Victoria Smith
W0403 Gary Sollars
W0404 Harlan Sparer
W0405 Rhiannon Sparer
W0406 Kellie Springer
W0407 James St. Andre
W0408 Ken St. Andre
W0409 Kevin Standlee
W0410 Patricia G. Steed (s)
W0411 E. L. Steglat
W0412 E. L. Steglat (g)
W0413 Alison Marie Stern
W0414 Katherine Stewart
W0415 Jim Strait
W0416 Edward Sulfaro
W0417 David Lee Summers
W0418 Chris Swanson
W0419 Gary L. Swaty
W0420 Paul Tanton
W0421 Sherilyn Thagard
W0422 Adam Tilghman (s)
W0423 Stephanie Timpany
W0424 (withheld)
W0425 Melissa Trible
W0426 Gene Turnbow
W0427 R-Laurraine Tutihasi
W0428 R-Laurraine Tutihasi (g)
W0429 Gerard Tyra
W0430 Sandra Tyra
W0431 Shawn Tyra
W0432 Susan Uttke
W0433 Billy Van Ark
W0434 Todd VanHooser
W0435 Tom Veal (s)
W0436 Illeana Vega Herrera
W0437 Julie Verley
W0438 Colette Vernon
W0439 Vixen's Cosplay Closet
W0440 Gregg Vohn
W0441 Mike Volckmann (s)
W0442 Elizabeth Vrabel
W0443 Denise Wallentinson
W0444 Paige Walters
W0445 Cynthia Ward
W0446 Cynthia Ward (g)
W0447 Thomas Watson
W0448 Ro Watts
W0449 Robin Ann Webb
W0450 Doreen Webbert
W0451 Jim Webbert
W0452 Stephanie Weippert
W0453 Lee Whiteside
W0454 Randall Whitlock

W0455 William B. Whitmore
W0456 Nadine Whitney
W0457 Nadine Whitney (g)
W0458 Bryan L. Wickham (s)
W0459 Mark N. Wickham (s)
W0460 Susan L. Wickham (s)
W0461 Courtney Willis
W0462 Mike Willmoth
W0463 Sally Woehrle
W0464 Travis Works
W0465 Austin Wright
W0466 Dania Wright
W0467 Natalie Wright
W0468 Ben Yalow
W0469 YaKnew, LLC
W0470 Misako Yamazaki
W0471 Catherine Yankovich (s)
W0472 Jerry Yeager
W0473 Lubov Yegudin (s)
W0474 Doug Young
W0475 Erica Young
W0476 Jennifer Zbylski
W0477 Connie Cockrell
W0478 Michael Brugger (s)
W0479 Karen Roop (s)
W0480 Catherine Roop (s)
W0481 Mariann Asanuma
W0482 October Art
W0483 Timothy Yamamura

Westercon History

We're proud to celebrate the 70th anniversary of Westercon, the sixth time it's been held in Arizona. More details are available at westercon.org.

#	Year	City (Name)	Chair (Org)
1	1948	Los Angeles, CA	E. Everett Evans (LASFS)
2	1949	Los Angeles, CA	Walter J. Daugherty (LASFS)
3	1950	Los Angeles, CA	Freddie Hershey (Outlanders)
4	1951	San Francisco, CA	Tom Quinn (Little Men)
5	1952	San Diego, CA (SouthwesterCon)	Roger Nelson
6	1953	Los Angeles, CA	E. Everett Evans, LASFS
7	1954	San Francisco, CA (SFCon)	J. Ben Stark
8	1955	Los Angeles, CA	Lew Kovner (Chesley Donovan Foundation)
9	1956	Oakland, CA	Marilyn Tulley
10	1957	Hollywood, CA	Lew Kovner, (LASFS/ Chesley Donovan Foundation)
11	1958	Los Angeles, CA (SolaCon)	Anna S. Moffatt (Outlanders)
12	1959	Seattle, WA	F. M. Busby (Nameless Ones)
13	1960	Boise, ID (BoyCon)	Guy & Diane Terwilliger
14	1961	Oakland, CA (BayCon)	Honey Woods (GGFS)
15	1962	Los Angeles, CA	Albert J. Lewis (LASFS)
16	1963	Burlingame, CA	Al haLevy (Little Men)
17	1964	Oakland, CA (PacifiCon II)	Al haLevy & J. Ben Stark
18	1965	Long Beach, CA	Steve Tolliver & John Trimble
19	1966	San Diego, CA	Dennis N. Smith
20	1967	Los Angeles, CA	Brandon Lamont
21	1968	Berkeley, CA (BayCon)	Bill Donaho, Alva Rogers & J. Ben Stark
22	1969	Santa Monica, CA (FUNCon II)	Chuck Crayne & Bruce Pelz
23	1970	Santa Barbara, CA	John & Bjo Trimble
24	1971	San Francisco, CA (SFCon '71)	Jerry Jacks
25	1972	Long Beach, CA	Dave Hulan
26	1973	San Francisco, CA (SFCon '73)	Jerry Jacks
27	1974	Santa Barbara, CA	Fred Patten
28	1975	Oakland, CA (OakLaCon)	Lois Newman & Craig Miller

#	Year	City (Name)	Chair (Org)
29	1976	Los Angeles, CA	Bruce Pelz
30	1977	Vancouver, BC	Fran Skene
31	1978	Los Angeles, CA (Westercone)	Ed Finkelstein & Mike Glyer
32	1979	San Francisco, CA	Jerry Jacks
33	1980	Los Angeles, CA	Milt Stevens
34	1981	Sacramento, CA	Michael Garrels
35	1982	Phoenix, AZ	Randy Rau (CASFS)
36	1983	San Jose, CA (Westerchron)	Lee Forgue
37	1984	Portland, OR	Steve Berry, Pam Davis & Bryce Walden (OSFCI)
38	1985	Sacramento, CA	Michael Garrels
39	1986	San Diego, CA	Gail Hanrahan, Mitchell Walker & Curtis White
40	1987	Oakland, CA (Episode X)	Lisa Deutsch Hannigan
41	1988	Phoenix, AZ	Terry Gish
42	1989	Anaheim, CA (Conosaurus)	Lex Nakashima & Patrice Cook (SCIFI)
43	1990	Portland, OR	Patty Wells & John Lorentz (OSFCI)
44	1991	Vancouver, BC	Terry Fowler
45	1992	Phoenix, AZ (Westercolt 45)	Bruce Farr
46	1993	Seattle, WA	Richard Wright
47	1994	Los Angeles, CA (Conozoic)	Noel Wolfman (SCIFI)
48	1995	Portland, OR	John Lorentz (OSFCI)
49	1996	El Paso, TX	Richard Brandt & Fred Duarte (SFFA/FACT)
50	1997	Seattle, WA	Sally Woehrle (SWOC)
51	1998	San Diego, CA (Concept 1998)	Dianna Hildreth (CAASM)
52	1999	Spokane, WA (Empirecon)	Bob Ladd (Team Maroon)
53	2000	Honolulu, HI (Conolulu)	Kathryn Daugherty (SFSFC)
54	2001	Portland, OR	Dean Koenig (OSFCI)
55	2002	Los Angeles, CA (Conagerie)	Bruce Pelz (SCIFI)
56	2003	SeaTac, WA	William Sadorus (SWOC)
57	2004	Litchfield Park, AZ (ConKopelli)	Craig Dyer (WesternSFA)
58	2005	Calgary, AB (Due North)	John Mansfield & Randy McCharles (CWSFA)
59	2006	San Diego, CA (Conzilla)	James M. Briggs (SDSFC)

#	Year	City (Name)	Chair (Org)
60	2007	San Mateo, CA (Gnomeward Bound)	Michael Siladi (SPFII)
61	2008	Las Vegas, NV	James Stanley Daugherty (Conventional Wisdom)
62	2009	Tempe, AZ (FiestaCon)	Mike Willmoth (Leprecon, Inc.)
63	2010	Pasadena, CA (Confirmation)	Christian B. McGuire (ISL)
64	2011	San Jose, CA	Glenn Glazer (SFSFC)
65	2012	Seattle, WA	Bobbie DuFault (SWOC)
66	2013	Sacramento, CA	Kevin Roche & Andy Trembley (SFSFC)
67	2014	Salt Lake City, UT	Dave Doering (CONduit SF&F)
68	2015	San Diego, CA	Ron Oakes (SanSFiS)
69	2016	Portland, OR	Lea Rush (OSFCI)
70	2017	Tempe, AZ (ConAlope)	Dee Astell (Leprecon, Inc.)
71	2018	Westminster, CO	Nikki Ebright (Shiny Garden)

Don't forget to vote at the Site Selection table in the Fan Tables area.

Utah for 2019 is the only bid for 2019.

utahfor2019.com

LepreCon History

As we're sponsored by Leprecon, Inc., we decided that Westercon 70 would be combined with our annual local convention, so we're also LepreCon 43.

#	Year	Chair	Venue
1	1975	Bruce Pelz	Quality Inn, Phoenix
2	1976	Greg Brown	Ramada Inn, Phoenix
3	1977	Barry Bard	Kachina & Thunderbird Lodges, Grand Canyon
4	1978	M. R. Hildebrand	Los Olivos Hotel Phoenix
5	1979	Ken St. Andre	Quality Inn, Phoenix
6	1980	Randy Rau	(canceled)
7	1981	Barry Bard	Caravan Inn, Phoenix
8	1982	Zetta Dillie	Caravan Inn, Phoenix
9	1983	Terry Gish	Ramada TowneHouse, Phoenix
10	1984	Pati Cook	Hyatt Regency, Phoenix
11	1985	Clif Baird	Hyatt Regency, Phoenix
12	1986	Terry Gish	Ramada Inn East, Phoenix
13	1987	Eric Hanson	Hyatt Regency, Phoenix
14	1988	Ray Gish	Hyatt Regency, Phoenix
15	1989	Sam Stubbs	Hyatt Regency, Phoenix
16	1990	Eric Hanson	Phoenix Sheraton, Phoenix
17	1991	Dave & Kim Hiatt	Safari Resort, Scottsdale
18	1992	Eric Hanson	Celebrity Hotel, Phoenix
19	1993	Doug Cosper	Camelview Resort, Scottsdale
20	1994	Pati Cook	(canceled)
21	1995	Dave & Kim Hiatt	Francisco Grande Hotel, Casa Grande
22	1996	Jay Patton	Francisco Grande Hotel, Casa Grande
23	1997	Charles Jarvis	Francisco Grande Hotel, Casa Grande
24	1998	Ray Gish	Francisco Grande Hotel, Casa Grande
25	1999	Pat Connors	Holiday Inn SunSpree Resort, Scottsdale
26	2000	Dave Hungerford	Holiday Inn SunSpree Resort, Scottsdale
27	2001	Mark Boniece	Holiday Inn SunSpree Resort, Scottsdale
28	2002	Lee Whiteside	Embassy Suites Phoenix North, Phoenix
29	2003	Shahn Cornell	Embassy Suites Phoenix North, Phoenix
30	2004	Mark Boniece	Sheraton Crescent Hotel, Phoenix

#	Year	Chair	Venue
31	2005	Larry Vela	Carefree Resort, Carefree
32	2006	Larry Vela	Embassy Suites Phoenix North, Phoenix
33	2007	Shahn Cornell	Phoenix Marriott Mesa, Mesa
34	2008	Liz Hanson	Francisco Grande Hotel, Casa Grande
35	2009	Ethan Moe	Phoenix Marriott Mesa, Mesa
36	2010	Lee Whiteside	Phoenix Marriott Mesa, Mesa
37	2011	Lee Whiteside	Tempe Mission Palms, Tempe
38	2012	Mark Boniece	Tempe Mission Palms, Tempe
39	2013	Donald Jacques & Patti Hultstrand	Phoenix Marriott Mesa, Mesa
40	2014	Donald Jacques	Phoenix Marriott Mesa, Mesa
41	2015	Paul Tanton	Embassy Suites Phoenix North, Phoenix
42	2016	Amanda Parker	Park Terrace Suites, Phoenix
43	2017	Dee Astell	Tempe Mission Palms, Tempe
44	2018	Michael Fett	Unexpected Art Gallery, Phoenix

Westercon 70 remembers ***Pati Cook****,*
Chair of LepreCon 10,
who passed on Thursday, June 8, 2017

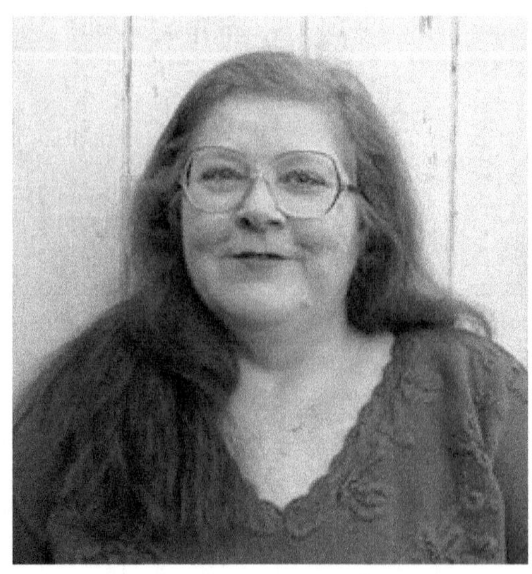

Arizona Fandom History

Arizona's fandom history has not yet been well documented, but its roots go back to the sixties when Westercon was a teenager who had only rarely ventured outside of California. These roots were varied.

Science fiction novelist Rick Cook founded a Phoenix chapter of the Society for Creative Anachronism in 1969 with Mike and Judy Reynolds. This grew into the Kingdom of Atenveldt that is still thriving today.

Our first convention was Phoenix Con in 1970, a comic book event run by Bruce Hamilton, a Scottsdale DJ, with Phoenix Comic Club members. Arizona's first guest was Carl Barks, creator of Scrooge McDuck. Phoenix Con returned in 1972 but was ironically never held in Phoenix!

Tucson fandom was soon spoiled for choice. A high profile movie con called Desertcon ran for most of the seventies at the University of Arizona with big budgets and major guests. Some committee members wanted a more personal event, so Jim Corrick and Carol de Priest founded TusCon in 1974, which is still going strong today as the oldest Arizona con still active. It's run by BASFA and Sue Thing has been a consistent chair since 1981.

Up in Phoenix, a core group of sci-fi fans grew out of meetings run by librarian Terry Ballard at Phoenix Public Library. They created LepreCon, named because the first event in 1975 was held over the St. Patrick's Day weekend. The United Federation of Phoenix was also founded in 1975 and both LepreCon and the UFP are still active today.

In addition to TusCon and LepreCon, Arizona in the seventies held all sorts of other fandom cons, often known by their nicknames rather than their usually unwieldy real ones: CookieCons, KandyKon, NoodleCon... the latter was held in Tucson in 1977, billed as 'the event of the millennium', which sounds like a fair description given who and what was there.

All this reached a pinnacle in 1978 when Arizona hosted the 36th World Science Fiction Convention. By all accounts, Iguanacon was enjoyed by attendees but it strained and broke friendships behind the scenes. Arizona fandom fractured and rebuilt. By the time Phoenix first hosted Westercon in 1982, new groups were in play. PhringeCon, Inc. hosted a couple of star-studded PhringeCons, with a strong *Star Trek* presence, and CASFS had started a long run of CopperCons, taking a focus on sci-fi literature after LepreCon had begun to focus on sci-fi art.

And so things continued for most of the eighties. Each year saw the trio of long-running Arizona sci-fi cons: LepreCon in the spring, CopperCon in the fall and TusCon a couple of months later. Interspersed among them were gate shows run by Creation Entertainment and others, which were usually dedicated to specific fandoms, mostly but not always *Star Trek*, and a growing collection of mobile cons, both regional and national.

Randy Rau chaired Westercon 35 in Phoenix in 1982 for CASFS. Terry Gish brought Westercon 41 back to Phoenix in 1988. In between, Rau also ran our first World Fantasy Convention in Tucson in 1985. Bruce Farr was the chair of the fourth NASFiC, held in Phoenix in 1987 when Worldcon was in England; he also chaired Arizona's only SMOFcon in 1988.

We've continued to host such events, of course. Leprecon, Inc. ran the first North American Discworld Convention in 2009. Arizona also hosted World Fantasy on two more occasions (in 1991 and 2004) and three World Horrors (in 1994, 1998 and 2004), as well as Costume-Con (in 2012) and the Browncoat Ball (in 2013). This is our sixth Westercon.

The local Arizona convention calendar started to busy up around the turn of the nineties with a variety of events filling a variety of niches. The first may have been CorsairCon, a pirate-themed event run by the Corsairs of the Desert Sea, Inc., though Bruce Farr's SmurfCon, a conrunners event, may predate it. Gaming events began with CASFS's HexaCon in 1991 and that ran for almost two decades. Henry Vanderbilt began his Space Access conferences in 1994 and that *has* run for two decades! The Dark Ones set up DarkCon in 1995, which is still active today. So is Doc Con, a Doc Savage event celebrating its 20th anniversary this year; that started in 1998, the same year as ZonieCon, the first Arizona con for the fur community.

Book festivals showed up in 1998 too, in multiple places. The Arizona Book Festival in Phoenix went on hiatus after ten events; the Tucson Festival of Books then took over and has become the largest fandom event in Arizona with attendance over 130,000 in each of the last four years.

The only other event to come close is Phoenix Comicon, founded and still run by Matt Solberg. It started in 2002 as Phoenix Cactus Comicon, a six hour comic book con in Ahwatukee; it topped 100,000 attendees in 2016. The Blue Ribbon Army, a non-profit social group which began as a Phoenix Comicon fan club, has 12,000 members on Facebook, making their conversation surely the most active that Arizona fandom has ever seen.

The fandom landscape has changed considerably over the decades, not least because what used to be niche is now the mainstream. PhringeCon, back in 1980, was 'for people interested in the fringes of science fiction', those fringes being fandoms like Marvel and *Star Trek*. Phoenix Comicon is the modern inheritor of PhringeCon's purpose as much as Phoenix Con's.

What's perhaps most notable is how the number of conventions held in state has grown. We may not have hit half a dozen in a year at any point during the seventies or eighties, but we reached double digits in 1998, then twenty in 2006, thirty in 2013 and forty in 2015!

Partly, this is because they represent a wide variety of fandoms: not just sci-fi cons, but anime cons, gaming cons, book cons, comic book cons, art cons, space cons, horror cons, fur cons, fanzine cons, faerie cons, dinosaur cons, collectible toy cons... you name it, we probably have it.

And partly, it's because mini-comicons are sprouting up in schools and libraries in cities across the state, where costs are low (or non-existent), staff are often inherent and events can be truly local. Instead of traveling to Phoenix and dealing with crazy crowds, many check out local events in San Luis, Apache Junction, Yuma, Cottonwood, Sierra Vista or Winslow. The pioneer here is Todd VanHooser, who has run Laughing Moon Con at Goodyear's Desert Edge High School since 2010.

— Hal C. F. Astell
Archivist, Arizona Penny Dreadfuls

If this has piqued your nostalgia, check out the Arizona Fandom History at azpennydreadfuls.org/azcons, with 3 GB of program books, PRs, flyers and other ephemera. And if you have anything that we don't, please let us know! This is a growing archive that would benefit from your memories!

Westercon Bylaws

As of Close of Westercon 69, July 4, 2016

The following document is the current text of the Westercon Bylaws and Standing Rules, as of the close of Westercon 69 (Portland, Oregon, 2016). No new amendments to the Westercon Bylaws were ratified at Westercon 69. Linda Deneroff and Kevin Standlee prepared this document based on the results of the Westercon 69 Business Meeting. With one item of business passed on to Westercon 69, the Bylaws were amended as shown below.

1. General Provisions

1.1 Name and Date

It is traditional, but not obligatory, that the West Coast Science Fantasy Conference (Westercon) shall take place over the July 4th weekend.

1.2 Guests of Honor

It is traditional, but not obligatory, that Westercon Guests of Honor and other notables be selected from among SF personalities residing within the Westercon geographical area.

1.3 Membership Classes

There shall be at least two classes of membership in Westercon: supporting and attending. The committee shall notify the members of their membership class in a timely fashion.

1.3.1 Supporting Members

Supporting members shall receive any progress reports or any other generally mailed publications published after the member joins the Westercon, including the Program Book, and may exercise any voting rights permitted by any other part of these bylaws, except attending the Business Meeting. All Westercons shall be required to offer supporting memberships until at least thirty (30) days prior to the opening of the Westercon, and such supporting memberships shall not cost more than one hundred and fifty percent (150%) of the voting fee charged when the site of the Westercon was selected. Any class of membership offered by a Westercon costing at least as much as a supporting membership shall include a supporting membership.

1.3.2 Attending Members

Attending members shall have all of the rights of supporting members, plus the right to attend the Westercon and the business meeting(s) held there, subject to the restrictions established by the other parts of these bylaws.

1.3.3 Restriction of Memberships

Each Westercon committee shall have the right to limit the activities of its attendees, either individually or in groups, insofar as such activities endanger, physically or legally, other persons or property. Such limitations may include, but are not limited to, closing down parties, ejecting persons from the Westercon, or turning offenders over to other authorities. No refund of membership need be given in such circumstances. Each member, in purchasing his/her membership, agrees to abide by these bylaws.

1.4 Name Badges and Membership Numbers

All committees shall issue name badges for all attending members. Name badges for pre-registered members shall display the member's name in no less than 24-point bold type. All committees shall assign a unique membership number upon processing of a membership. This number provided to each member with the site selection ballot and with each progress report, shall be printed on membership name badges, and shall be used for site-selection purposes. In the event a membership is transferred, the old membership number, if applicable, shall be noted, both on the badge and on registration information used for site-selection voting administration. Membership badges or other proof of membership remain the property of the Westercon committee for the duration of the conference and may be confiscated for cause; no refund of membership fees need be given in such circumstances.

1.5 Archive of Bylaws

The Los Angeles Science Fantasy Society, Inc. (LASFS) shall act as an archive to the Westercon bylaws and the minutes of business meetings. Each committee shall reimburse LASFS for the costs of copying and forwarding copies of the Bylaws and Minutes to those who request them. A copy of the minutes, including the text of motions passed by the business meeting, shall be sent to LASFS within two (2) months of the close of each Westercon by the administering Westercon. LASFS shall maintain the Westercon bylaws and shall forward one copy of the current bylaws, including the text of any amendment to the bylaws awaiting secondary ratification, to the current Westercon committee within four (4) months of the close of the previous Westercon. The current Westercon shall provide copies of the Bylaws to the committees of all Westercon bids for the year which that Westercon is administering the site-selection.

1.6 Distribution of Bylaws to Members

The Westercon Bylaws, as well as the complete text of any amendment awaiting secondary ratification, shall be published in at least one (1) progress report and in the program book of the current Westercon each year. Failure to publish this information shall not affect the procedure to amend the bylaws as stated in Article 4.

1.7 Westercon Service Mark

All Westercons shall publish, in all publications such as promotional flyers, progress reports, and program book, the following notice: "'Westercon' is a registered service mark of the Los Angeles Science Fantasy Society, Inc."

1.8 Responsibilities of Administering Westercon

It is a responsibility of each Westercon to enforce the provisions of these bylaws.

1.9 Committee Failure

Should a Westercon Committee declare itself unable to fulfill its duties, the Board of Directors of the Los Angeles Science Fantasy Society shall determine alternate arrangements for that Westercon.

2 Westercon Business Meeting

2.1 Scheduling of Sessions

At least one (1) regular session of the Westercon business meeting must be scheduled at each Westercon. No regular session of the Westercon business meeting shall be scheduled to start prior to 11 AM, nor later than 2 PM, nor on the last day of the Westercon. A special session, at which site-selection business shall be the sole order of business, may be scheduled on the last day of the convention, provided that said special meeting is scheduled to begin no earlier than 11 AM or later than 2 PM. All sessions occurring during the same Westercon, be they regular, adjourned, or special, shall be considered, for procedural purposes, as the same parliamentary session.

2.2 Site-Selection Business

Site-selection business shall be in order at any session of the business meeting. Site-selection business shall include, but need not be limited to, the announcement of the results of the balloting and of a winner if one is produced by the balloting, or of a site-selection resolution, as hereafter defined, if one is necessary [see Section 3.16]. The winner of the site-selection may be announced prior to the site-selection business meeting, if one is held.

2.3 Quorum

For business other than site-selection business, a quorum of ten (10) attending members of the current Westercon shall be required. For site-selection business, the quorum shall be those attending members of the current Westercon who attend the meeting. All those persons voting at any meeting must be attending members of the current Westercon. Except as noted in these bylaws or in such rules of order as may be adopted, all business requires a simple majority to pass.

2.4 Parliamentary Authority

The current edition of *Robert's Rules of Order Newly Revised* shall be the parliamentary authority of the Westercon business meeting except where it conflicts with these bylaws or with any special rules of order which may be adopted by the business meeting.

3 Westercon Site-Selection

3.1 Eligibility of Sites

Any site on the North American continent west of the 104th west meridian, or in the state of Hawaii, shall be eligible to be the site of a Westercon, except as restricted by the provisions of these bylaws.

Provided that, upon the annexation of Australia by the United States of America or the annexation of the United States of America by Australia, Section 3.1 shall be amended to read:

"Any site in Australia, or on the North American continent west of the 104th west meridian, or in the state of Hawaii, shall be eligible to be the site of a Westercon, except as restricted by the provisions of these bylaws."

[Note: On a parliamentary inquiry based on a question of when the annexation must take place for a site to be eligible, the 2002 Business Meeting decided that a bid for an Australian site is eligible, even if the annexation has not yet taken place, provided that the annexation has taken place by the filing deadline for the intervening Westercon (the April 15th following the Westercon at which the Australian Westercon is selected), and that if the Australian site has been selected, and the annexation has not taken place by that date, then this shall constitute committee failure, as covered by Section 1.9.]

3.2 Site Selection Zones

The following Site Selection Zones are defined within the area defined in section 3.1:

3.2.1: North: Sites in North America north of the 42nd north parallel.

3.2.2: Central: Sites in North America between the North and South zones.

3.2.3: South: Hawaii; California south of and including San Luis Obispo, Kern, and San Bernardino Counties; Nevada south of and including Clark County; Arizona; New Mexico; and all countries, states, provinces, territories, or other political subdivisions southward within North

America.

3.2.4: Other: Any location otherwise eligible under section 3.1 not part of the above zones.

3.3 Regional Exclusion Zone

No site within the Site Selection Zone containing the site of the Westercon administering the site-selection election shall be eligible to bid, except as provided in this section. If no eligible bids are filed by the January 1st of the year of the site-selection balloting, then all sites defined in section 3.1 shall be eligible.

3.4 Filing Deadline for Ballot

Only those eligible bids whose filing paperwork required by section 3.5 is in the possession of the administering Westercon by the April 15th preceding the balloting shall be listed on the ballot.

[Note: On a parliamentary inquiry at the time of ratification of the text of the above section, it was ruled that "If the filing paperwork can be verified to be at the address of the administering convention, it is in the committee's possession."]

3.5 Filing Requirements

A Westercon bid committee must provide written evidence of the following: At least two (2) separate people declaring themselves Chairman and Treasurer; an organizing instrument such as bylaws, articles of incorporation or association, or a partnership agreement; and a letter of intent or option from a hotel or other facility declaring specific dates on which the Westercon shall be held; and, for a sponsoring organization from within the United States of America, evidence that the sponsoring organization is a non-profit association or corporation within the applicable state law of the sponsoring organization.

3.6 Eligibility of Voters

Site-selection voting shall be limited to those persons who are attending or supporting members of the administering Westercon and who have paid a voting fee toward their membership in the Westercon being selected. Other classes of membership may vote only upon the unanimous agreement of all qualified bidding committees. One person equals one membership equals one vote. Corporations, Associations, and other non-human entities may vote only for "No Preference." "Guest of" memberships must be transferred to an individual before voting for anything other than "No Preference."

3.7 Voting Fee

The voting fee shall be twenty US dollars (US$20.00) or the local equivalent unless the committees listed on the ballot and the administering Westercon agree unanimously to charge a different amount.

3.8 Minimum Rights of Voters

The payment of the voting fee shall make the voter at least a full supporting member of the Westercon being selected, and may make the voter an attending member at the discretion of the winning bid.

3.9 Prototype Ballot

The Los Angeles Science Fantasy Society, Inc. (LASFS) shall prepare a prototype site-selection ballot, including instructions for preparation of the ballot, and shall provide the prototype to each administering Westercon at the same time the bylaws are provided to the administering Westercon as provided for in section 1.5. Upon receipt of the prototype, the administering Westercon shall complete the ballot by filing in the information about the eligible bid committees, including the dates of the proposed Westercons, the voting fee, minimum membership requirements, including the cost of a supporting membership in the administering Westercon, and the address to which site-selection ballots should be sent. The administering Westercon shall be responsible for the publication and the distribution of the ballots to the membership of the administering Westercon. All eligible bids received in accordance with sections 3.4 and 3.5 shall be included on the ballot. The ballot shall also include entries for "No Preference" and "None of the Above," and shall provide space for at least one (1) write-in bid. The ballot shall be a secret ballot, specially marked for preferential voting with an explanation of the method of counting preferential votes.

3.10 Distribution of Ballot

The site-selection ballot and full rules for site-selection voting, including the deadlines for voting by mail, shall be mailed on or before the May 10th preceding the voting to all members of the administering Westercon as of one week before the mailing. The ballot and full rules for site-selection, including the hours during which site-selection will take place and the location of the site-selection, shall be given to all attending members upon registration at the Westercon, or such information shall be prominently displayed at the registration area throughout the Westercon.

3.11 Deadline for Voting by Mail

All ballots received by the administering Westercon prior to June 20 shall be counted.

3.12 Bid Presentations

Each eligible bid committee shall have at least fifteen (15) minutes of scheduled program time on the first full day of the administering Westercon for the purpose of making a bidding presentation.

3.13 At-Conference Voting

Site-selection shall be open for at least six (6) hours between the hours of 11 AM and Midnight on the day before the business meeting at which site-selection business is scheduled. All on-site balloting shall be from one central location, under the supervision of the administering Westercon. If no site-selection business meeting is scheduled, then site-selection shall be open for at least six (6) hours between the hours of 11 AM and Midnight on the next-to-last day of the administering Westercon.

3.14 Verification of Ballots

Properly completed ballots shall contain: the member's printed name; the member's membership number as assigned by the administering Westercon; the member's dated signature; the member's address of record with the current Westercon; the member's current address if different; and the member's vote(s) as defined elsewhere in this article. Verification of the ballots shall consist of matching the name and number of the member with the records of the administering Westercon. Ballots received by the committee prior to June 20, and any others received by mail which may be counted, shall be held by the administering Westercon until the opening of the Westercon, at which time they shall be verified by the administering Westercon and the bidders.

3.15 Counting of Ballots

The administering Westercon shall arrange for the counting of ballots, and each eligible bid committee shall be allowed to send at least two (2) observers to such ballot-counting. The count shall be by preferential ballot. The winner shall be that bid which gains a majority of those votes expressing preference for a bid. For the purpose of vote counting, "None of the Above" shall be treated as if it were a bid. "None of the Above" and votes for ineligible bids shall count toward the total number of votes cast. Blank ballots, illegal or illegible ballots, and votes for "No Preference" shall not count toward the total number of votes cast. All vote totals of final results and of all intermediate counts shall be made available at or before the closing ceremony.

3.16 Procedures When No Bid Wins or is Eligible

Should no eligible bid gain the needed majority, or should there be no qualified bidding committee, or should "None of the Above" win, a three-fourths (3/4) majority of the site-selection business meeting of the administering Westercon may award the Westercon to any bid, or a simple majority of the meeting may decide that they are unable to decide. If the business meeting does not choose a site, the Board of Directors of the Los Angeles Science Fantasy Society, Inc. shall choose a site within six (6) weeks of the close of the administering Westercon. If "None of the Above" wins, none of the bids which were on the ballot may be selected. A site chosen under the provisions of this section shall not be restricted by any portion of this article except this section and section 3.1.

3.17 Availability of Results

The results of the balloting shall be reported to the site-selection business meeting of the administering Westercon, if one is held. A record of the results of the balloting, including all intermediate counts and distinguishing between the by-mail and at-con ballots, shall be published in the first or second progress report of the winning Westercon.

3.18 Hand-Carried Ballots

The administering Westercon shall accept hand-carried ballots, which are otherwise valid ballots delivered to the administering Westercon by someone other than the member who prepared the ballot.

4 Procedure for Amendment of These Bylaws

4.1 Method of Adoption

Amendments to the Westercon Bylaws must be ratified by the majority vote of the business meetings in two consecutive years. Proposed amendments shall be read in full by the chairman of the business meeting immediately before being voted upon.

4.2 Primary and Secondary Ratification

The secretary of the business meeting at which an amendment receives primary (first year) ratification shall submit an exact copy of the amendment to the following year's Westercon business meeting. The question of secondary (second year) ratification is debatable and is amendable only to the extent that such amendments do not increase the scope of the original bylaw amendment.

4.3 Effective Date of Amendments

Unless otherwise provided, amendments shall take effect at the close of the Westercon where they receive final ratification. Operating rules for already-selected Westercons shall not be changed by amendments to the bylaws. Rules regarding eligibility and voting procedures for site-selection are not considered to be operating rules.

Standing Rules

1. Close Debate. Before proceeding to take a vote on a motion for the Previous Question, the presiding officer shall ask for a show of hands of how many people still wish to speak to the pending motion. This rule does not allow debate on the motion for the Previous Question.

Business Passed On and Draft Agenda for Westercon 70

1. Call to Order

2. Committee Reports

There are no active committees of the Business Meeting.

3. Pending Bylaw Amendments

No new Amendments were adopted at Westercon 69 therefore nothing needs to be ratified at Westercon 70.

4. New Business

Bylaws amendments passed by the Westercon 70 Business Meeting will be passed on to the following year's Westercon for ratification.

5. Announcements

6. Adjournment

The above copy of the Bylaws, Standing Rules, and Business Passed On of the West Coast Science Fantasy Conference is hereby certified to be true, correct, and complete, effective as of the close of Westercon 69, July 4, 2016.

Kevin Standlee, Chairman
Linda Deneroff, Secretary
Westercon 69 Business Meeting

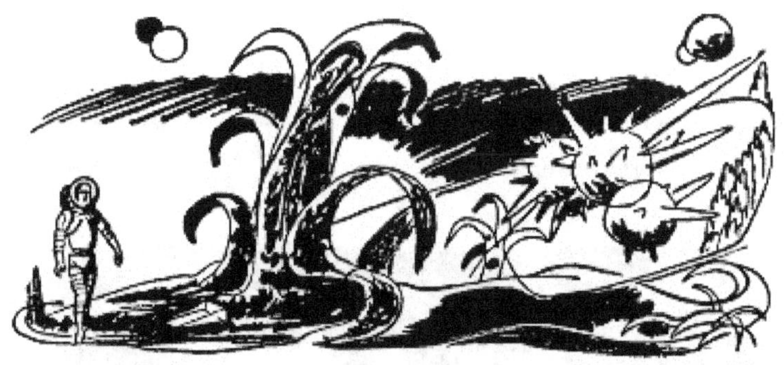

Advertisements

We thank our advertisers, whether paid or swapped.

BayCon 2018 (p52)	baycon.org
Book Gallery (p41)	alibris.com/stores/bookgallerymikeriley
Collectors Marketplace (p41)	collectorsmarketplace.com
Del Rey Books (p19)	unboundworlds.com
The House of Freaks (p178)	thehouseoffreaks.com
Imperial Outpost Games (p65)	imperialoutpostgames.com
Isle of Games (p62)	isleofgamesaz.com
Left Hand Asylum (p115)	lefthandasylum.com
LepreCon 44 (p181)	leprecon.org
Loscon 44 (p59)	loscon.org
LTUE (Life, the Universe and Everything) (p29)	ltue.net
MileHiCon 49 (p51)	milehicon.org
NESFA Press (p136)	nesfa.org/press
Orycon 39 (p49)	39.orycon.org
Frankie Robertson (p107)	frankierobertson.wordpress.com
Samurai Comics (p50)	samuraicomics.com
Trash City Beads (p27)	trashcity.com
TusCon 44 (p86)	tusconscificon.com
Utah for 2019 (iv)	utahfor2019.com
Thomas Watson (p112)	underdesertstars.wordpress.com
Westercon 71 (i)	westercon71.org
WesternSFA (p23)	westernsfa.org
Wild Wild West Steampunk Convention (p160)	wildwestcon.com
Worldcon San Jose 208 (p22)	worldcon76.org

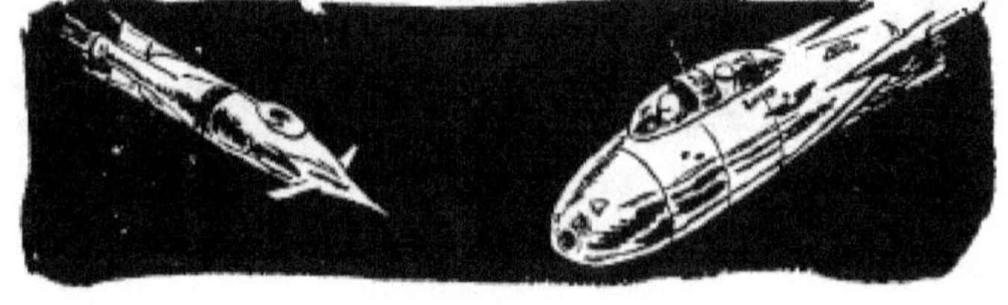

Image Credits

pp12-13	photos (c) the respective individuals except Val & Ron Ontell, photo courtesy of Dee Astell
p15	images (c) Julie Dillon
p16	photo courtesy of Hal C. F. Astell
p21	photo courtesy of Marsheila Rockwell
p25	photo courtesy of Dee Astell
p31	image (c) Larry Elmore
p32	photo courtesy of Dr. Dave Williams
p34	photo courtesy of Leprecon, Inc.
pp54-58	posters (c) the respective filmmakers
p65	image by n4pgamer (public domain)
pp120, 139	images by kellepics (public domain)
p148	image by unknown creator (public domain)
p155	image by mindofmush (public domain)
p167	*The Flying Carpet* by Viktor Vasnetsov (1880)
p198	image by tombud (public domain)

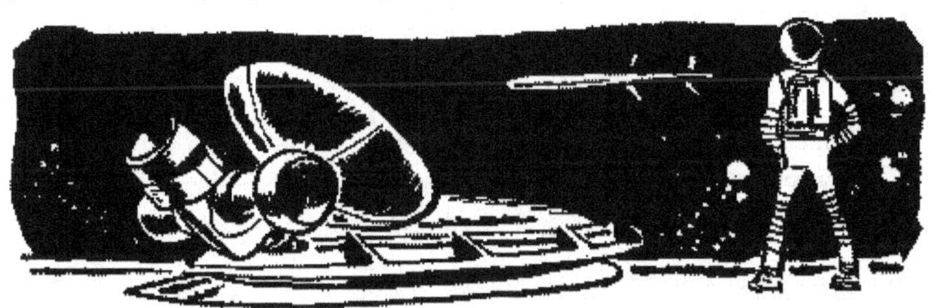

Line art by Louis Glanzman, from *Tom Corbett: Space Cadet* novels
(all in the public domain):
from *Danger in Deep Space* (pp117, 123, 154, 195, 197)
from *Sabotage in Space* (pp43, 45, 131, 197)
from *The Space Pioneers* (pp73, 130, 147, 196)
from *Stand by for Mars!* (p89)
from *Treachery in Outer Space* (pp28, 71, 124)

Staff List

Westercon 70 was brought to you by...

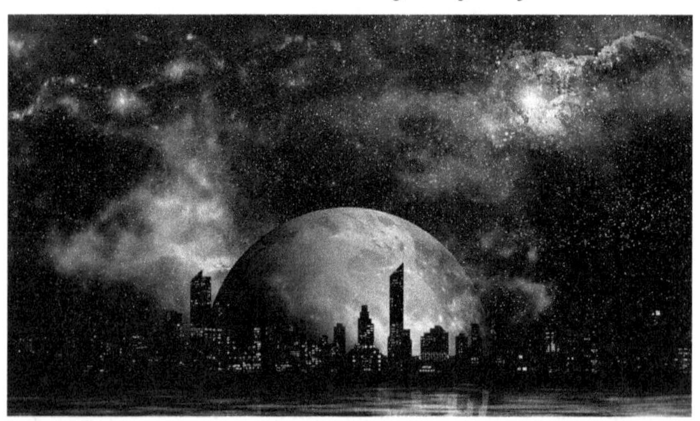

Executive Team

Chair	Dee Astell
Vice Chair	Hal C. F. Astell
Treasurer	Kevin McAlonan
Hotel Liaison	Mark Boniece

Department Heads

Art Show	David Gish and Annette Sexton-Ruiz
Ambience	Margaret Grady
Dealers' Room	Mark Boniece
Gaming	Earl C. Hedges
Guest Liaison	Kate Hatcher
Hospitality	Wendy Trakes
Operations	Paul Tanton
Party Maven	Mark Boniece
Programming	Michael Flanders
Publications	Hal C. F. Astell
Publicity	Deb Krol
Registration	Deena Johnson
Sponsorship	Kate Hatcher and Dee & Hal C. F. Astell

Staff

Dealers' Room	
On Site-Liaison	Duncan Rittschof
Hospitality	Kevin Hull and Alice Massoglia
Operations	
Fan Tables	Marcus Johnston
Logistics	Michael Flanders, Shawn Flanders and Jaziel Molina
Operations Room	Mandy Parker
Rangers	Victor Bugg
Signage	Woody Bernardi
Volunteers	Dawndreia Robinson
Programming	
Art	Dee Astell
Books and Authors	Michael Senft
Dances	Alex Canto
Diversity	Jen McAlonan
Fandom	Hal C. F. Astell
Filk	Valerie Richie and Gary Swaty
Film	Jon Bonnell
General	Michael Flanders
Masquerade	Elaine Mami
Moderation	Edward Pulley
Post-Con Events	Hal C. F. Astell
Science	KellyAnn Bonnell and Dee Astell
Steampunk	Dee Astell
Publicity	
Social Media	Dee Astell
Publications	
Marketing/Graphics	Jason Drotman
Marketing/West Coast	Anastasia Hunter
Website	Diane Shreve (creator/designer) Hal C. F. Astell (webmaster)

That's it. It's over. Go home. But we hope to see you next year!

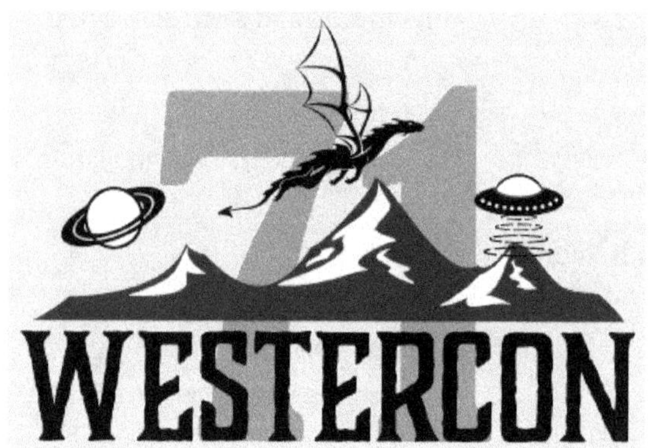

Westercon 71 will be in Westminster, CO from July 4th to 8th, 2018.
It'll be run by Shiny Garden, with Nikki Ebright the chair.
It'll also be Myths & Legends (MALCon) 6.
Check out details at westercon71.org.

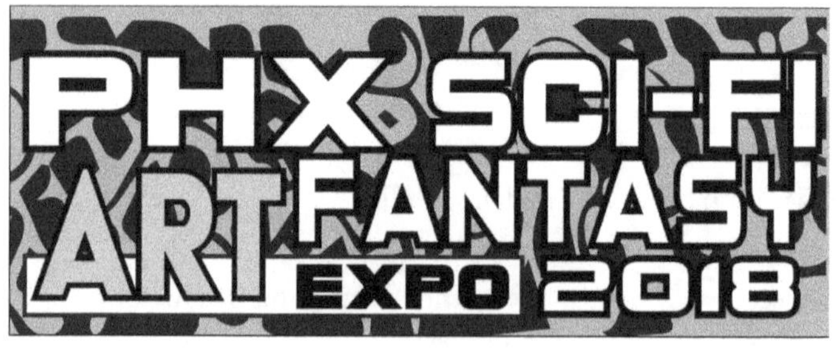

LepreCon 44 will be in Phoenix, AZ from March 16th to 18th, 2018.
It'll be run by Leprecon, Inc., with Michael Fett the chair.
It'll be branded as the Phoenix Sci-Fi and Fantasy Art Expo.
Check out details at leprecon.org.

www.ingramcontent.com/pod-product-compliance
Lightning Source LLC
Chambersburg PA
CBHW060844170526
45158CB00001B/226

9780989461351